Antebellum Slave Narratives

Studies in American Popular History and Culture

JEROME NADELHAFT, *General Editor*

For a full list of titles in this series, please visit www.routledge.com

Antebellum Slave Narratives

Cultural and Political Expressions of Africa

Jermaine O. Archer

Routledge

Taylor & Francis Group

New York   London

First published 2009
by Routledge
711 Third Ave, New York, NY 10017

Simultaneously published in the UK
by Routledge
2 Park Square, Milton Park, Abingdon, Oxon OX14 4RN

First issued in paperback in 2013
Routledge is an imprint of the Taylor & Francis Group, an informa business

© 2009 Taylor & Francis

Typeset in Sabon by IBT Global.

Library of Congress Cataloging in Publication Data
Archer, Jermaine O.
   Antebellum slave narratives : cultural and political expressions of Africa / by Jermaine O. Archer.
      p. cm.—(Studies in American popular history and culture)
   Includes bibliographical references and index.
   1. Slave narratives—United States—History and criticism.   2. American literature—African American authors—History and criticism.   3. Pan-Africanism in literature.   4. Africa—In literature.   5. Africa—Social life and customs.   6. Africa—Politics and government.   I. Title.
   E444.A73 2009
   306.3'62092—dc22
   2008036728

ISBN13: 978-0-415-84609-7 (pbk)
ISBN13: 978-0-415-99027-1 (hbk)
ISBN13: 978-0-203-88168-2 (ebk)

Contents

Preface

TOUSSAINT, the most unhappy man of men!
  Whether the whistling Rustic tend his plough
  Within thy hearing, or thy head be now
  Pillowed in some deep dungeon's earless den;
  O miserable Chieftain! where and when
  Wilt thou find patience? Yet die not; do thou
  Wear rather in thy bonds a cheerful brow:
  Though fallen thyself, never to rise again,
  Live, and take comfort. Thou hast left behind
  Powers that will work for thee; air, earth, and skies;
  There's not a breathing of the common wind
  That will forget thee; thou hast great allies;
  Thy friends are exultations, agonies,
  And love, and man's unconquerable mind.

—William Worsdworth, "To Toussaint L'OVERTURE," 1803.[1]

When Arna Bontemps wrote *Black Thunder* (1936), a historical novel based on the 1800 Virginia slave conspiracy led by Gabriel Prosser, he must have had William Wordsworth's poem in mind when he titled the fourth section of the book "A Breathing of the Common Wind."[2] Wordsworth, a renowned poet of the English Romantic movement, opposed what he believed to be an oppressive French aristocracy and was a staunch supporter of the 1789 Revolution that toppled the regime.[3] His poem *To Toussaint L'OUVERTURE* reveals that he championed the leader of the related Haitian (formerly San Domingo) rebellion of 1791 in which blacks successfully overthrew the French Army and established the first black republic in the Americas. The Jacobin tradition, the radical faction of the French Revolution, bequeathed its political principals to the Haitian dissenters and it was reported that some of the Jacobin immigrants also had a hand in Gabriel's scheme. It is this connection of ideological parallels between the movements that Bontemps explores in *Black Thunder*.[4]

Bontemps was inspired to write the book after combing through the slave narrative collection held at Fisk University in Nashville, Tennessee during the 1930s. He became fascinated with the accounts of slave resistance and was particularly intrigued with Gabriel Prosser.[5] Bontemps's literary treatment of the plot seems to suggest that "a breathing of the common wind" may have also been a reference to the shared African cultural currents between the people of San Domingo and the slaves of Virginia. It was rumored that the Haitian revolution was successful because the insurgents engaged in African ritual by sacrificing a pig and drinking the blood to ensure their victory.[6] Bontemps's Gabriel, on the other hand, distanced himself from the African beliefs and rituals of his community and a number of his coconspirators were convinced that such neglect prevented the successful execution of their plot.[7]

While the conspiracy became unraveled when two slaves of a neighboring plantation disclosed its details to their masters, even Gabriel ultimately attributed the collapse of the scheme to his failure to ritualistically acknowledge the gods and take heed to the "signs" that the stars were not in his favor. Insurgents worried that Gabriel did not spiritually arm himself as "Toussaint over yonder in San Domingo" had. They believed that if Gabriel had only accepted the protective charms fashioned by conjure doctors and interpreted the poor weather conditions as divine caveats, he might have achieved his goal. His decision to distance himself from some of the African beliefs and rituals of his community resulted in the fateful demise of his plot.[8]

Given the widespread descriptions of African culture located within antebellum slave narratives, particularly those published during the Garrisonian abolitionist movement, it is small wonder that Bontemps, an exceptional scholar on the narrative, includes this material in *Black Thunder*.[9] References to the belief in protective talismans to ward off physical and spiritual danger are found throughout a number of slave narratives.

Bontemps also hints that he understood the centrality that the ring shout, one of the many common African cultural threads linking the narratives of Frederick Douglass, William Wells Brown, Harriet Tubman, and Harriet Jacobs, had to black spiritual expressions. Describing the galvanization of the rebels, one of Bontemps's characters says, "they'll drop out of the sky when they hears sticks a-cracking together and drums a-beating. They'll come shouting like jackals and hyenas."[10] Perhaps Bontemps was thinking of Douglass's recollections of hearing a wild hoarse laugh emerge from a circle of dancers on his Maryland plantation or of Brown's telling account of the ring shout ceremonies he witnessed in St. Louis, New Orleans, and Tennessee. Or maybe he drew from the North or South Carolinian examples offered by Jacobs and Tubman. Bontemps certainly had ample examples from which to choose.

The slave narratives in what becomes the United States are among the most compelling sources for examining the slaves' remembrance of Africa. This investigation is a meditation on the common cultural and political winds between slaves and their African forebears and contemporaries. While there are over six thousand extant narratives spanning from 1703 to 1944, the most significant literary period of the genre occurred between 1836 and the 1860s. The narratives of the eighteenth and early nineteenth centuries tend to focus on the theme of adventure as the authors were primarily concerned with providing accounts of their own individual escape.[11]

With the growth of Garrisonian abolitionism in the 1830s the tone of the slave narratives shifted. Since the texts were now being financed and produced by a Garrisonian-influenced anti-slavery press, the authors were given greater leverage to express a class consciousness. No longer did they have to be silent about the hypocrisy of southern religion or minimize the wrongs that had been committed against them. This period ushered in a new wave of what may be referred to as "radical narratives" as the authors not only called for the preservation of an anti-slavery Christianity and questioned the morality of the slave-owning class, but also relayed their connections with African culture.

The narratives are not texts of cultural discontinuity and disruption.[12] Rather they are treatises on anti-slavery politics with underlying expressions of cultural memory. This project devotes specific attention to the narratives of Douglass, Brown, Tubman, and Jacobs because these individuals not only left us with their rich memoirs, but they also became well- known activist reformers who offered keen observations on African cultural while moving in highly visible political circles.

The first chapter lends close attention to the cultural and political attitudes found in the three narratives of Frederick Douglass. Not only does he offer insightful commentary on religion, dance, and conjuration within the slave quarters, he also straddled the political fence. Douglass has often been considered a moderate assimilationist. Yet, his writings and speeches also demonstrate a political and social "radicalism" that was intrinsic to his character. While Douglass may have at times realized the practical need to dismiss the value of African culture given both contemporary perceptions and his exalted status as an advocate for abolitionism he still in subtle and even explicit ways demonstrated an appreciation for African culture and a desire to bring down the slave power by any measure of resistance necessary. This along with his critique of southern religion and his tendency to differentiate between the Christianity of the slaves and that of the master class makes Douglass an even more complex figure than we have imagined.

The second chapter provides a similar assessment of William Wells Brown who, like Douglass, has often been considered a moderate integrationist. Brown's texts offers a unique perspective to the popular book-length narratives of the nineteenth century because his cultural views on culture and radical political ideas can be examined in light of his other writings. Brown was the only author of slave narratives to also write histories, novels, and dramatic pieces and the chapter on him raises the query of how each of these genres substantiate or refute the themes he addresses in his narrative.

The third and fourth chapters probe the slave narratives of two of the most renowned women of the slavery era—Harriet Tubman and Harriet

Jacobs respectively. Tubman is by far the most noted woman of the slave class. However, little has been written on her beyond the genre of juvenile literature. It is suggested in the third chapter that Tubman's association with the biblical figure Moses was not limited to her role as "liberator." Relying on the anthropological and historical writings of Zora Neale Hurston and others who have explored the conjurational nature of Moses in the black folk tradition as one who is often associated with African deities, this chapter concludes that Tubman as a seer, self-proclaimed communicant with God, and root-worker represented Moses in the fullest sense of African-American spiritual constructions.

The fourth chapter on Jacobs examines her remarkable references to pharmacopoeia methods that mirrored African healing techniques. Significant attention is also given to her intriguing remarks on visions and of the annual John Kunering parade in North Carolina. While various forms of Kunering have been documented in regions throughout the African Diaspora, scholars agree that the festival was confined to North Carolina in the United States. It is postulated here that the parade may have extended to South Carolina. This chapter also endeavors to answer the question of whether or not the appropriation of the Canoe or houseboat in the Kunering festival had something to do with escape or the idea of returning back to Africa.

The final chapter shows how my research fits within the larger historiographical discussion on the slave narrative and the abolitionist movement. I offer a new interpretation on U.S. anti-slavery ideology by arguing that African attempts to thwart the Atlantic slave trade, such as the marabout movement of seventeenth-century Senegambia, which spurred a string of resistance movements in the region throughout the eighteenth century, must be considered when examining the foundations of abolitionism.

The slave narratives not only reflect the individual lives of those few persons fortunate enough to tell their stories but also serve as critical sources for the slave community as the authors tell of their experiences with slaves across plantations and states, thus making this project more than an intellectual analysis of a select few who had the opportunity to use such mediums. These memoirs are much more than tales of bondage and freedom. Indeed, they are vital tools for all students of African-American folklore and, as will be argued, for uncovering African cultural continuities. When one wonders how slaves endured their condition, an important part of the answer can be found in the slaves breathing of the common African wind that is found throughout the slave narrative.

Acknowledgements

One of my earliest and fondest childhood memories is of my grandmother opening the wooden chest that my Uncle Bruce had brought back from his travels in Africa and fortuitously retrieving its items and placing them before me to let me make of them what I would. Her fascination with its treasures was matched by my youthful intrigue. The multi-colored garments, hand crafted statuettes and masks, and glimmering jewelry were enough to make any five-year-old feel as though they had encountered a vast wealth of play objects that could lead them on a journey beyond their imagination. The subtle and unassuming dialogue of cultural instruction from the senior matriarch of my family marked the early beginnings of my understanding of who I was and from whom I had come. In many ways the relationship resembled the connection between Frederick Douglass and his grandmother Betsy Bailey, and Harriet Jacobs and her grandmother Molly Hornblow. Much like Betsy and Molly, my grandmother offered valuable lessons of history and genealogy by making me aware that the continent from which my ancestors originated was graced with a profound stroke of intellectual and artistic genius that was as great as any on the globe.

My conception of Africa was never remote or intangible largely because of Uncle Bruce's voyage across the Atlantic and my grandmother's commitment to see to it that I embarked on the same journey as far as a young lad could without boarding a plane. Before I realized that I was the descendant of slaves, I knew that I was the descendant of Africans. I am beholden to my grandmother and other family members for planting the seeds that have shaped my passion for African-American history.

I am particularly indebted to my dear mother Cheryl Archer, a native of the Bronx, New York who is of the folk and for the folk. Her strength and straightforwardness have sustained me. It was my mother's love for books that instilled in me a thirst for knowledge. Her children's happiness has always been her primary concern and for that I am grateful. My father Bernardo Archer, an Afro-Costa Rican of Jamaican decent, exemplifies the leadership and promise of the working class. His dedication to the plight of dock workers and laborers on banana plantations instilled in me a desire to give voice to the downtrodden. While working on this project he shared with me his remarkable knowledge of African culture in Latin America and the British Caribbean.

The work ethic of my siblings Jeff, Junior, Tanya, and Octavius inspires me to push forward. I am thankful for their examples of consistency and dedication. My wonderful relatives, the Singleton family of Boston, have always opened their hearts and it is in large part to them that I owe my sense of extended kinship. My loving mother-in-law, Vicki Springer, has made sure her home is my home. Her thoughtfulness is humbling.

Among noteworthy colleagues and friends who have shared insightful ideas about this project are Sterling Stuckey, Michael Gomez, Douglass Daniels, Ray Kea, Ralph Crowder, Daniel Black, Rinaldo Murray, Aubrey Bonnett, Rosalyn Baxandall, Elizabeth Ewen, Amanda Frisken, Anya Dennis, Kenya Casey, Jason Young, Walter Rucker, Rahel Kassahun, Ramona Washington, Kwakiutl Dreher, Angie Beatty, and Dean Rodrigues. While a list of all my family members and peers would be too lengthy to include here, I wish to thank them for their encouragement whenever appropriate. I *am* because you *are*.

I extend a most special note of appreciation to my wife Celeste and our daughter Sanaya. Celeste has provided unparalleled companionship, understanding, and support. Her drive and inner strength are amazing to observe. I honor Celeste with deep gratitude for the selfless nurturer that she is. I know of no one with a purer and kinder spirit. Even at her young age Sanaya's zeal and priceless smile serves as a constant reminder that the tender simplicities of life are indeed its miracles. She is our joy.

1 "Speaking Guinea and a Mixture of Everything Else"

The Slave Narratives of Frederick Douglass Revisited

From both a literary and historical standpoint, Frederick Douglass authored the most significant full-length slave narratives of the nineteenth century. The sales of his memoirs were higher than any other slave narrative and the publication of the first edition, *Narrative of the Life of Frederick Douglass, an American Slave, Written by Himself* in 1845, marked a watershed in the abolitionist movement. The American public learned in fine detail the story of those held in bondage from a former member of the slave class who exceeded all literary expectations and was rapidly gaining momentum as a formidable force in abolitionist circles. The second version, *My Bondage and My Freedom*, appeared in 1855 and was succeeded by Douglass's final narrative, the *Life and Times of Frederick Douglass, Written by Himself*, printed in 1881 and reprinted again in 1892 and 1893. Each of the three narratives progressively elaborated on Douglass's experiences as a slave and eventually a free man.

Regarded as the nineteenth-century exemplar of black genius, Douglass's writings have generally led scholars to draw one-sided conclusions regarding his spiritual views and cultural influences. It has been assumed that he was not cut from the same revolutionary cloth of some nineteenth-century black radicals and that he thoroughly embraced the culture of the majority population in lieu of drawing on that which was rooted in any African tradition.[1] However, through his autobiographies Douglass emerges as a multifaceted character whose intimate familiarity with the slave community and views of intra-group solidarity and resistance were deeply entrenched in his character. While Douglass benefited from the comparatively better lot as an urban skilled slave in Baltimore, he was exposed to the harsher life of a plantation laborer in rural Maryland. These experiences along with his journey to eventually becoming one of the foremost orators on abolitionism both in the United States and abroad, ultimately contributed to how Douglass would come to interpret the world.

Unlike their more moderate abolitionist predecessors of the late eighteenth century, Garrisonians disagreed with the idea that slavery should come to a gradual end. Since clerical leaders were not fighting for its instant removal, Christian institutions became prime targets for criticism.

Garrisonians considered slavery a sin and were convinced that the most efficient means to rid the United States of this social wrong was through moral suasion as opposed to political action, the latter only serving to validate a pro-slavery union and its constitution.[2] Early on in his career Douglass, like most Garrisonians, favored integration. While he initially rejected the more radical nationalist pleas of David Walker's 1829 anti-slavery *Appeal to the Colored Citizens of the World* and Henry Highland Garnet's 1843 *Address to the Slaves of the United States of America*, Douglass demonstrated shades of radicalism throughout his narratives and became increasingly radical after the enactment of the 1850 fugitive slave law.[3]

While Christianity had a profound impact on Douglass, it was not the only source of theology and culture for him. Douglass's revealing discussion of his maternal grandmother, the languages and dialects spoken by slaves, the work skills he encountered on Maryland plantations, slave manners and social relations, his observations on dancing rituals and conjuration, along with his own perception of Christianity, plantation paternalism, and slave resistance locate Douglass within the broader scope of African culture. The contours of these themes and their sometimes fluid nature will be explored in this chapter.[4]

Benjamin Quarles broke ground when he wrote Douglass's first biography in the late 1940s. Nearly twenty years would pass before Phillip Foner published the second biography on Douglass. Indeed Quarles and Foner present solid accounts. Neither, however, seemed interested in Douglass's observations on slave culture. Quarles's primary concern was to insert Douglass in the annals of American history. Foner reasoned that a wide gap existed between Douglass and the masses of black people because he did not break ties with the republicans and align himself with the labor party after reconstruction failed. Waldo Martin Jr. and Dickson Preston agreed in the early 1980s that Douglass's intellectual and cultural roots could only be found in Protestant Christianity and the Enlightenment. Denying that he was influenced by African culture, Preston like Foner argued that Douglass always found it difficult to relate to large segments of the black population.[5]

The tendency to portray the authors of slave narratives as passive historical subjects who, more often than not, only sought and desired the spiritual direction of whites runs counter to their writings. Douglass's narratives presents evidence that disputes the notion that the blacks who participated in the antebellum political arena and authored slave narratives were hardly purveyors of African culture. Our aim here is to show how Frederick Douglass and others were indeed able to assert their own voice within the abolitionist literary power structure.[6]

Some of Douglass's earliest memories were of his grandparents Betsy and Isaac Bailey with whom he resided until the age of seven in humble quarters in Talbot County Maryland. Betsy Bailey looked after several of her grandchildren until they were able to yield a significant profit. While Douglass's mother was virtually a stranger to him, he admitted that his lot was far better than those unfortunate souls who were placed in the hands of strangers instead of having the privilege of intimately knowing their blood relatives. [7] While he did not disclose much about his grandfather who was a free man, Douglass related that Betsy Baily was known for her expertise in catching fish with her own specialized crafted nets, enjoyed the reputation of being a first rate midwife and was well versed in the manipulation of *roots*. It was believed by the slaves at the Holme Hill Farm in Talbot County Maryland that "Grandmother Betty was born to good luck." Douglass would often find her with her intricately woven nets in the water for half of the day. He knew of no one who could boast of catching greater quantities of shad and herring. [8] Many of the local slaves were convinced that Betsy Bailey's touch alone would assure a fruitful crop and it was for this reason that many flocked to her during harvest season to have their sweet potatoes planted by her in the hills. She knew how to care for the root in such a way as to prevent it from damage. Those under her care, especially Douglass, appreciated the value of being kin to one so distinguished. [9]

Betsy Bailey's status as a "gifted" agriculturalist was likely informed by West African harvest rituals. Similar views were popular throughout much of the region. The Bight of Biafra, which comprises contemporary southeastern Nigeria, Cameroon and Gabon, was responsible for contributing the largest imports of slaves to Maryland. Igboes and Ibibios from the Nigerian region became the largest cluster of Africans in the state. [10] Of the Ibibio, Percy Talbot observed a harvest ritual that occurred during the sowing of yams in which people came to seek protection and bountiful harvest. The high priest would mark the attendees with a white chalky substance to indicate that they came to the festival to receive the promised blessing. [11] The Gold Coast, which is made up of present day Ghana, supplied the second largest group of slave imports to Maryland and Robert Rattray observed three festivals among the Ashanti that revolved around the harvest season. A.B. Ellis witnessed similar yam festivals of the Tshi-speaking peoples of the Gold Coast that honored the gods for looking after the crop. [12]

The African-American community of Talbot County Maryland was the recipient of African labor skills and spiritual views associated with these crafts. Given Douglass's accounts of African languages and the ring shout in the Talbot County region and the notion that Betsy Bailey had a magical green thumb of some sort, it is fair to speculate that she probably engaged in both African linguistic patterns and cultural dance practices.

Douglass's master Aaron Anthony, who might have been his father, was the superintendent and clerk on the main estate belonging to Edward Lloyd located on the Wye River twelve miles outside of Holme Hill Farm. Anthony summoned Douglass to relocate there in 1824. Up until that point, his grandmother had served as his only nurturer and protector. He knew of no higher authority than her and the young Douglass was deeply saddened when he was forced to part with his treasured matriarch whom he likened to that of a priestess when he described her special agricultural "touch." Douglass was impressed with her physical strength and her graceful countenance. "My grandmother, though advance in years," he says "as was evident from more than one gray hair, which peeped from between the ample and graceful folds of her newly ironed bandana turban—was yet a woman of power and spirit. She was marvelously straight in figure, elastic, and muscular. I seemed hardly to be a burden to her." She was his foundation and his strength. In her he found love, guidance, and protection. Though he was perhaps too young to learn how to make the well-designed fishnets used to retrieve shad and herring from his grandmother or how to become provident in the preservation of seedling sweet potatoes, Douglass enjoyed the privilege of first learning about life from his cherished "grandmammy."[13]

Edward Lloyd owned thirteen farms and close to a thousand slaves. Significant numbers of Africans and first generation American-born slaves lived on his plantation. They wielded significant influence on the young Douglass, thereby helping ease the social transition from his grandmother's quarters to the Lloyd residence.[14] Indeed, there was much with which Douglass was not familiar on the estate. He had not seen this many children before nor had he encountered so many laborers in the field. "All this hurry, noise, and singing was very different from the stillness of Tuckahoe."[15] The main agricultural products on the farm were tobacco, corn, and wheat. The core plantation supplied the mechanical labor for its peripheral farms of Wye Town and New Design.

Like Betsy Bailey at the Holme Hill farm, a number of Lloyd's slaves were versed in skilled trades. These included shoemaking and mending, blacksmithing, cartwrighting, coopering, weaving, and grain grinding.[16] Caste systems throughout much of Africa were comprised of endogamous occupational groups trained in such trades. Michael Gomez explains that among these groups were "blacksmiths, *griots*, woodworkers, potters, weavers, and leatherworkers."[17] Douglass was perhaps the first from the slave class to identify the ways in which these arrangements might have taken shape in the nineteenth century:

> "Uncle" Toney was the blacksmith, "Uncle" Harry the Cartwright, and "Uncle" Abel was the shoemaker, and these had assistants in their several departments. These mechanics were called "Uncles" by all the younger slaves, not because they really sustained that relationship to any, but according to plantation etiquette, as a mark of respect, due from the younger to the older slaves.[18]

From such etiquette, Douglass concluded that "there is no better material in the world for making a gentleman than is furnished in the African."[19] Here Douglass links the slaves' esteemed deference for senior slaves who mastered particular skills with African social norms. While craft guilds in

Africa were often kept in tact through familial lines, Douglass's account of the widespread use of the term "uncle," used even if there were no actual blood ties, suggests that African kinship associations though sometimes fictive were reinforced in America.

Douglass also spoke favorably of Uncle Isaac Cooper, another one of the "slave notabilities" who also practiced conjuration while remaining attentive to all who sought his counsel. That he was a cripple did not prevent Uncle Cooper from effectively serving as a doctor of medicine and divinity to the slaves on the Lloyd plantation. "His remedial prescriptions embraced four articles. For diseases of the body, *Epsom salts* and *castor oil*; for those of the soul, *the Lord's Prayer,* and *hickory switches!*"[20] These relationships were particularly important given the disruptive and precarious nature that slavery had on the black family.[21] Even though the older slaves were subject to their masters' every whim and will the younger ones did not fail to recognize their rank. The same respect was accorded to Betsy Bailey as she was familiarly referred to as "Grandmamma Betty." Those who were advanced in years had much to teach the youth. Some of this instruction as in the case of work skills took place openly and in plain view of the master while a great deal of what they offered the generation that followed occurred behind closed doors.[22]

Much of the training that took place between those at the top of the craft hierarchy and their apprentices relied heavily on African languages or an Africanized form of English. Douglass is quite instructive on the vernacular spoken by the slaves on Lloyd's estate, which was related to the singing and instrumentation that accompanied their dancing rituals. He claimed that the Lloyd plantation had the characteristics of a small nation with a language of its own.[23] The choruses of the slaves' songs reverberated like "unmeaning jargon" to outsiders who lent their ears. To the singers themselves, however, the meaning was crystal clear—slavery must end:

> I did not, when a slave, understand the deep meaning of those rude and apparently incoherent songs. I was myself within the *circle*; so that I neither saw nor heard as those without might see and hear. They told a tale of woe which was then altogether beyond my feeble comprehension; they were tones loud, long, and deep; they breathed the prayer and complaint of souls boiling over with the bitterest anguish.[24]

Considering both the attention that Douglass devotes to circular dance and song in his writings and the prevalence of ring shout ceremonies in nineteenth-century Maryland and throughout the rural south for that matter, it is probable that his reference to being "within the circle" refers to the ring shout. An African-influenced spiritual and religious articulation, the ring shout encompasses single file counter-clockwise circular movement, song, and the rhythmic trudging and pattering of one's feet—all of which sought the desired purpose of invoking and or appeasing the ancestors and deities. The cadence and orbit of the ring gradually increases as the ceremony persists and as the intensity and enthusiasm heightens, spiritual "mountings" or ecstatic seizures are in accordance with the accepted norms of the ritual. The church along with makeshift places of worship like the "brush harbor" frequently housed ring shout gatherings. Slaves also took to the open fields to enjoy a "shout." To be sure, the dance was ubiquitous throughout much of the African Diaspora.[25]

Circle dance varied across the African regions from which captives originated. Yet its centrality of ancestral reverence and invocation remained in tact throughout the Americas. Sterling Stuckey argues that it was the strongest common thread which aided Africans in the process of transcending ethnic and religious differences throughout the slave era in North America and in-turn paved the way for an emerging single African-American identity. The ring shout was the primary vehicle for the Africanization of Christianity that made its way into the slave quarters and the main components lasted well after slavery ended. Bishop Daniel Alexander Payne of the African Methodist Episcopal Church (A.M.E.) offered his accounts of the strong presence that the ring shout had in even the urban areas of Maryland during the second half of the nineteenth century. Hence, it should not surprise us that Douglass while still a slave would have observed and even participated in the ring shout in rural Maryland.[26] The Lloyd plantation was very much an African linguistic and cultural enclave and Douglass may have quickly learned that an important spiritual exercise of its inhabitants was the ring shout.

According to Douglass, it was not uncommon for one to "hear a wild, hoarse *laugh* arise from a *circle*, and often a song" when the slaves were allowed a brief amount of leisure time following their evening meals.[27] Writing of the ceremonies he observed while traveling in Cairo Douglass says "the dancing and howling *dervishes* often spin around in their religious transports till their heads lose control and they fall to the floor sighing, groaning, and foaming at the mouth like madmen, reminding one of scenes that sometimes occur at our old-fashioned camp-meetings." Douglass displayed an interest in the similar phenotypical and cultural traits that existed among Egyptians and blacks in the United States. Never hesitant to exalt the "great" civilization of ancient Egypt, he concluded its inhabitants were a "Negroid" people. It is quite significant then that Douglass, who was often classified as an integrationist and thus lacked an African cultural awareness, established a connection between the dances of Egypt and those he observed in the south.[28] Douglass's use of the word "dervishes" to describe these dances is also employed in a number of nineteenth-century sources. In 1863 Lucy Chase who worked as a surgeon in the 18th Massachusetts Infantry and served as Superintendent of Negro Affairs under General Butler wrote of her superior Dr. Orlando Brown: "He loses no opportunity to impress upon the noisy worshippers that boisterous Amens, wild, *dancing-dervish* flourishes—'Oh that's the

Devil,' exclamations—. . . and pandemoniamics generally do not constitute religion."[29]

Douglass provided a more detailed and explicit description of the ring shout in *Life and Times*. He may have become more comfortable with discussing such practices that were largely considered heathenish well after slavery was abolished. As a visible proponent of the abolitionist movement, he recognized the pragmatic need to convince people that the abject conditions of slavery worked against the permeation of white cultural influences and Christian moral standards within the slave community. If his reading and listening audience were convinced that slavery fostered practices believed to be immoral, it could only help to convey the message that the institution should be abolished. Still, while abolitionism remained his primary objective, he was hardly guilty of having rejected his Africanness.

The idea of defying perceptions of cultural and intellectual inferiority had been with Douglass at least since the summer of 1841. It was during these months that he began touring with high-ranking members of the Massachusetts Anti-Slavery Society with the purpose of both soliciting subscriptions for the *National Anti-Slavery Standard* and *The Liberator* and lecturing at local anti-slavery conventions. Douglass's abolitionist friends encouraged him to refrain from coming across in his speeches as *too* articulate and erudite. He was to be regarded as mere chattel and nothing more. For he was of the slave class and few if any of his new found comrades saw the political value in having a great mind among their ranks who was of such a "low origin." Thus, he was urged not to offer an extensive critique of slavery, but rather to simply provide the facts and leave the philosophy to those of a lighter hue. They told him "better to have a *little* of the plantation manner of speech than not;' tis not best that you seem too learned."[30] Those he traveled with wondered why Douglass did not speak like the other slaves. When his full discussion of the African vernacular that he heard and spoke is weighed alongside his reflections on black inferiority it appears that Douglass cleverly sought to appease his fellow slaves who spoke the languages and embraced black culture while concurrently satisfying those who looked down upon them. Again, such ambiguity served as a means to an end—the abolishment of slavery.[31]

What he tells us of the coded language used by him and his cohorts during their unsuccessful attempt to escape in 1836 demonstrates an early ability to strategically disguise his true intent. They had a comprehensive secret communication network that was completely undecipherable to outsiders.[32] Their own vernacular tradition was responsible for clandestine acts of small-scale resistance, which in this instance was flight. Since Douglass imagined that on no other plantation would one hear as much altered English infused with African languages and linguistic patterns as was heard on the Lloyd estate, their expressions were undoubtedly heavily imbued with African syntax and dialect.[33]

When Douglass gave the commencement speech to the Literary Society of Western Reserve College in Hudson, Ohio in 1854 entitled *The Claims of the Negro Ethnologically Considered*, he touched upon the relationship between the linguistic patterns of the Egyptians and other peoples throughout Africa with the dialects and various tongues he listened to while he was a slave. His address marked the first time that a black person was selected to be the keynote speaker at a major university and Douglass sought to demonstrate that those of the slave class were not that different from the esteemed Egyptians of antiquity at a time when the latter were largely considered distinct from African Americans. Following his discourse on the physical commonalities between the two groups he conveyed his belief that the trained philologist would recognize "equal similarity in the structures of their languages."[34] He went on to say

> Language is held to be very important, by the best ethnologists, in tracing out the remotest affinities of nations, tribes, classes and families. The color of the skin has sometimes been less enduring than the speech of a people. I speak by authority, and follow in the footsteps of some of the most learned writers on the natural and ethnological history of man, when I affirm that one of the most direct and conclusive proofs of the general affinity of Northern African nations with those of West, East and South Africa, is found in the general similarity of their language[s].[35]

Douglass also attacked ethnologist Charles Hamilton Smith's conclusions that "the typically woolly haired races have never discovered an alphabet, framed a grammatical language, nor made the least step in science or art." In Douglass's rejoinder to Smith, he mentioned a Mandingo man "of the Western coast of Africa, who has framed an alphabet." Though he understood how Smith might have been ignorant of this particular fact, Douglass believed "as an ethnologist, he is inexcusable for not knowing that the Mpongwe language, spoken on both sides of the Gaboon River, at Cape Lopez, Cape St. Catherine, and in the interior, to the distance of two or three hundred miles is as truly a grammatically framed language as any extant." [36]

Douglass also refuted claims of black inferiority in an address he gave to the Massachusetts Anti-Slavery Society on January 26, 1865 entitled *What the Black Man Wants*: "I utterly deny that we are originally, or naturally, or practically, or in any way, or in any important sense, inferior to anybody on this globe."[37] He spoke to the American Anti-Slavery Society in New York later that year and again harked backed to his feelings on the connections between Egyptians and blacks residing in the United States. He noted that "Ethiopia" was at its cultural and intellectual height when Europe "floundered in the depths of ignorance and barbarism." He spoke of the impressive examples of Egyptian architecture and of the superior nautical, military, commercial and mechanical skills that they once possessed. He reiterated "we are a dark people—so were they." He professed that the influences of Egypt could be found in contemporary West Africa, Haiti, and among blacks at home. To corroborate his assertion that West Africa had been stroked with the brush of Egyptian greatness he cited the accounts of Heinrich Barth, David Livingston, and John Leighton Wilson, all of whom were nineteenth-century travelers to Sub-Saharan Africa.[38]

Douglass concluded that Africans were essentially one people whereby each "tribe bears an intimate relation to other tribes and nations in that quarter of the globe, and that Egyptians may have flung off the different tribes seen there at different times, as implied by the evident relations of their language, and by other similarities." While Douglass may not recognize important differences between African ethnicities, his Diasporic and Pan-African view to connect West African and African-American culture and history to those of the Egyptians reflected his strong desire to prove that African Americans deserved an equal footing with whites.[39] Offering a lesson on the structure of the *different* English spoken by the slaves on the Lloyd plantation Douglass explained that they were not prone to include the "*s*" when employing the possessive tense. "Cap'n Ant'ney Tom," for example, actually meant "Captain Anthony's Tom." "*Oo you dem long to?*" served as a substitute for "Whom do you belong to?" and "*Have you got any peaches?*" was replaced by "*Oo dem got any peachy?*"[40]

It is this same vernacular tradition that has given rise to the linguistic patterns found in slave spirituals, tales, narrative poems, verbal games, jokes, the blues, sermons, jazz, poetry, and even contemporary hip hop and rhythm and blues music.[41] Blacks were able to maintain a sense of group unity and cohesion through these linguistic expressions. The common thread running throughout each of these oratorical expressions was and still is the goal of "verbal creativity" and secrecy.[42] Generally, persons who were far removed from or existed outside the core black community were unable to fully grasp the meaning. In fact, when Douglass first arrived on the Lloyd estate there was much that he could not decipher and he was convinced that the slaves' "broken" speech could only serve to hinder him intellectually. Little did he know that he would eventually come to depend on this "mixture of Guinea and everything else" to help him escape. Douglass first encountered this speech through the slave songs by which he was so deeply moved. Though Douglass appears to be somewhat embarrassed by the language he hears, his confession that his abolitionist colleagues did not want him to come across as *too* intellectual must have contributed to his uneasiness.[43]

Lorenzo Dow Turner's research on the South Carolinian Sea Island Gullah and Geechee linguistic forms demonstrates that the African elements of their dialects continued at least a half-century following emancipation. Much like the Maryland slaves who Douglass writes about, the peoples of the Sea Islands also employed a completely different vocabulary and syntax when speaking to those outside the group. The comprehension of intra-group dialect and or language was usually reserved for blacks.[44] Nonetheless, as Douglass makes clear, there were times when whites, particularly children, were exposed to and even embraced the speech patterns of slaves.

Douglass's white childhood playmate *"Mas'* Daniel," son of Colonel Lloyd, was greatly influenced by the African vernacular spoken by the slaves. He was Douglass's closest companion during his youth and he not only picked up the dialect of the slaves but also absorbed their notions of time and space. Douglass pens: "The equality of nature is so strongly asserted in childhood and childhood requires children for associates. *Color* makes no difference with a child." Given the pervasiveness of African dialects and languages spoken on the plantation along with the large numbers of slaves that came directly from Africa we can conclude that the sounds of Africa that resonated throughout the Lloyd estate not only shaped the young Daniel but also had an influence on Colonel Lloyd and the other adults.[45] There has been little discussion by scholars on the subject of cultural influences that blacks had on whites. It is generally assumed that African culture was obliterated by the nineteenth century and thus slaves were simply unable to share what they no longer possessed. Douglass's revelation then begs the question of how this transmission of culture might have served to reinforce its persistence among blacks themselves. If Daniel soaked up linguistic and cultural aspects from the numerous Africans and first-generation American-born slaves who resided on his father's estate, Douglass, in addition to learning the "proper" way to speak from Daniel, was also probably able to strengthen his connection to African culture from him and other whites who were colored by it.[46]

Theologist and literary critic, Theophus Smith, views the African-American magical folk tradition of conjuring culture and performance as a language of ritual speech through which slaves were able to communicate with one another. He says magic is thought of as the way by which people are able to affect and control their reality through the form and interpretation of corresponding signs. That is, a particular action yields a specific result. Smith's theoretical framework can be applied to the writings of Frederick Douglass and other authors of slave narratives who touched upon African culture and spirituality in their texts.[47] Smith does not view conjuration as a function of irrational thought and behavior that should be simply assigned to the sphere of the supernatural or the unconventional domain of the occult. Rather he sees it as a viable system of communication by which the descendants of Africans were able to express themselves through this magical scheme of correspondences. The conjure culture of slaves was not one that revolved around the sole purpose of witchcraft and malign sorcery. Conjure culture in the African-American sense is defined as the process by which the healing or exacerbating of one's condition is possible through the operation and invocation of exceptional powers. According to Smith, herein lies the distinction of the slave conjure tradition. This dual aspect of the conjure doctor's ability to heal and or harm through pharmacopoeial methods including the use of herbs, roots, and human artifacts reflects the balance that is intrinsic to the African magician and medicinal doctor.[48]

Smith has proposed a rather broad context for understanding conjure performance among African-Americans. It is his contention that conjuring culture should not only be viewed through the lens of folklore practices but also through the effort to initiate social–historical transformations. He has outlined three instances in which these transformations take place. These include "ritually patterned behaviors and performative uses of language and symbols," the intent to heal or harm through pharmacopeic methods, and the use of biblical figures and appropriating biblical configurations to fit one's cultural experience. Concerning the use of the Bible to identify these transformations Smith directs us to the work of Folklorist Zora Neale Hurston and folklore archivist Harry Hyatt. Hurston included the Bible in her list of the "paraphernalia of conjure" and Hyatt has found the text to be used "as a talisman or amulet, on the one hand, and a source of conjurational spells, incantations, or prayers on the other."[49]

We can explore Douglass's experiences and interactions with pharmacopeic methods and his discussion of Christianity and the bible in light of Smith's formulation of conjuring culture. When Douglass's master retired from the Lloyd estate in 1826 his slaves were forced to leave. Douglass went to live with Hugh and Sophia Auld in the Fells point district of Baltimore.[50] Hugh Auld was the brother of merchant and postmaster Thomas Auld, the latter of whom was married to Lucretia Anthony, the daughter of Douglass's master. In March of 1833 Thomas Auld requested that Douglass be returned to his quarters in the St. Michaels region of Talbot County because he thought Douglass would prove more profitable if he hired him out. On January 1, 1834 Douglass was sent to work for Edward Covey to labor on his 150-acre farm that he rented from Edward Lloyd on the northwestern outskirts of St. Michaels. While working on Covey's estate Douglass became the victim of the constant floggings for which Covey was notorious and by the summer months he had had enough when he received a vicious beating for simply fainting from heat exhaustion while carrying wheat. This prompted him to run off to St. Michaels to inform Thomas Auld that if he were not removed from the Covey residence he would be killed. Unconvinced that his investment in Douglass's labor was actually in jeopardy Auld tried to reassure him that his worries were exaggerated and demanded that he return to Covey's farm in the morning. When he returned the next day Covey chased him while chastising him for leaving the estate without his consent.[51]

Determined to evade Covey this time, Douglass sought refuge in a nearby cornfield. He then made his way to a wooded area and was greeted by Sandy Jenkins an "old adviser" who was also of the slave class. Sandy was in route to see his wife and when he learned of Douglass's trials he invited

Douglass to accompany him. While at the home of his wife, Sandy suggested that before Douglass's return to Covey's farm he procure a special root from a particular area in the woods. Sandy told him that if he wore it on his *right* side no white man including Covey could whip him. Sandy explained that he had not received a flogging while carrying it nor did he ever expect he would.

Initially doubting its effectiveness, Douglass was not inclined to retrieve the talisman. Yet Sandy spoke of them with such passion and conviction that Douglass, aiming to please the wise elder, decided to test their worth. When Douglass arrived home on Sunday morning with the roots on his person he was surprised by Covey's cordialness. He reasoned that such an attitude might very well have had something to do with Sandy's prescription. However, Covey's pleasantness was short-lived. The slave breaker took occasion to assault him the following day, at which time Douglass was filled with an unshakeable spirit to fight back against his tormentor. Unlike previous scuffles, Covey was unable to punish Douglass this time. In fact, it was Covey who sustained considerable injuries. This event was a turning point in Douglass's life. From this moment on he no longer endured a whipping from Covey or any other person. Moreover, he related how he went through a sort of rite of passage under Sandy's tutelage. "You have seen how a man was made a slave," he says "you shall see how a slave was made a man."[52] Such were his feelings after defeating Covey while holding on to the roots. Douglass wondered if the spirit within the root was ruled by a divine presence. "How did I know but that the hand of the Lord was in it?" he writes, "with thoughts of this sort, I took the roots from Sandy, and put them in my right hand pocket." He goes on to say, "My religious views on the subject of resisting my master, had suffered a serious shock, by the savage persecution to which I had been subjected, and my hands were no longer tied by my religion."[53] Covey was a class leader in the Methodist church and Douglass was determined to reject the obedient servant motif that was perpetuated by him and other slaveholders.

Though Douglass may have not wholeheartedly embraced Sandy's prescription or at least admit that he had, it still played a significant role in the transformation of his religious views. It should not be lost on us that Sandy's magical talisman affected this social change within Douglass. Sandy's intent was to heal and protect his patient through an age-old African pharmacopeic method. Douglass was quite candid about the personal spiritual renewal that he underwent as a result of the extraordinary powers that Sandy evoked. His social reality was changed by the belief that Sandy, a gifted conjure doctor, had the ability to effect change through his root remedies.

Commenting on Sandy's spiritual views Douglass alleged that he was a religious man who "had inherited some of the so called magical powers, said to be possessed by African and Eastern nations."[54] The two often mused over Douglass's success over Covey. Sandy, "a clever soul," would always attribute the victory to the roots. Instructive on the pervasiveness of this sort of belief within the slave community, Douglass admitted that "this superstition is very common among the more ignorant slaves. A slave seldom dies but that his death is attributed to trickery."[55] If Douglass truly believed that Sandy was ignorant, such sentiments did not prevent him from planning an escape with him and four other conspirators in 1836. That he wanted to include Sandy, the man "of root memory" who played a significant role in his transition to manhood as part of his plot to flee is evidence of both Douglass's deep affection towards Sandy of whose inveterate African sensibility Douglass was altogether aware.[56]

Douglass would have been wise to have heeded the warning signs that came to Sandy through a dream during the planning of their escape. They prevented the conjure doctor from following through with the plot. Sandy dreamt of birds seizing Douglass during his attempted flight and was convinced that it was a bad omen.[57] Douglass initially dismissed Sandy's intuitive experience as little more than a frivolous premonition. Yet he ultimately concluded that had he acted on his deep feeling that Sandy was right, he and the other slaves—there were four in number—would not have been apprehended and sent to the Easton county-seat jail on the morning of April 2 after the plot was uncovered.

Again, Douglass conceded the authenticity of Sandy's gift: "As I looked upon this crowd of vile persons, and saw myself and friends thus assailed and persecuted, I could not help seeing the fulfillment of Sandy's dream. I was in the hands of moral vultures, and firmly held in their sharp talons." Dreams were and continue to be an extension and manifestation of the culture of African-American conjurers. It was believed that through them the future was vividly foreseeable. They served as signs of what was to come in the physical world. The slave community relied on them as a sort of life roadmap to prevent particular things from occurring or to interpret that which was not fully understood in the conscious state. Unlike the occasion when he took Sandy's advice regarding the Covey incident, Douglass's decision not to listen to the wise oracle on this occasion worked against him.[58]

Because of Sandy's extensive knowledge of the escape plan, his visionary insight, and his decision not to participate, he seemed a likely suspect in the scheme's betrayal. However, Douglass noted that he and the others were unable to point the finger at old man Sandy Jenkins. "We could not suspect him," they reasoned, "We all loved him too well to think it possible that he could have betrayed us. So we rolled the guilt on other shoulders." For them, the matter was quite simple; Sandy, "a genuine African," and first-rate conjure doctor was too influential and highly regarded to have unwavering doubt cast upon him. Contrary to the claim that Sandy informed Douglass' negative impressions of Africa, Douglass expressed the utmost respect for the conjurer who emerged as a hero more often than not.[59]

When Douglass addressed the New York State Vigilance Committee on May 8, 1849 at J. W. C. Pennington's Shiloh Presbyterian church he again spoke quite fondly of Sandy to whom he was thankful for also instilling in him the art of "thievery." The speech was entitled *Shalt Thou Steal?* It was a response to a popular debate of the day on whether or not slaves were morally just in stealing from their masters. Douglass began the speech by expressing his feelings on the slaves' right to seize their freedom. He conveyed that he was much in favor of running away—for he could see no legitimate reason why slaveholders would seek claim over another's arms, feet, and legs. Such an entitlement he felt was against God's will. Douglass then briefly mentioned his own spiritual awakening that occurred when he was about twelve years old. He recalled being taught two of the more popular religious messages of contemporary southern Christianity. These were that slaves should unconditionally obey their masters and refrain from stealing. Douglass then went on to inform his audience that it was around this time that his views on stealing became qualified from an insightful conversation he had with Sandy:

> I dared not to talk to any of the delinquency of eatables on the plantation but to one, a confidant named Sandy Jiggins [Jenkins], and to him I poured forth the pithy strains of an empty stomach—he was a religious, kind soul, and in our conversations he said to me, "Why is it that you never have any money?" I answered, "I toil from morning till night—from Monday morn till Saturday night and part of the Sunday, and my master has all the gains of my toil." "Well," said Sandy, "you must think for yourself." At length said he, "You must learn to steal something to eat, you mustn't be hungry—aye, I could steal a pig—blessed be God—and shout hallelujah!" "How do you justify that Sandy?" asked I. "Well,?" "Well, you master's property too." "Yes." "Well, then suppose you put some of that master's property into this—it would only, in the language of Gen. Jackson, be a question of removal!"—and, friends, ever after I had plenty of pig.[60]

Sandy's performative use of religious language instilled upon Douglass that stealing from slave owners was not against God's will and served to once again enact a personal social–historical transformation within Douglass. As mentioned earlier, he admitted that Sandy was influenced by African spirituality. Since this is not the only instance in which he avers that Sandy was a man of religion corroborates the notion that though many whites considered religion and African spirituality to be diametrically opposed, they were not on opposite ends of the spectrum in Douglass's view.

In *Life and Times*, Douglass provides a compendium of his tenure as president of the Freedmen's Savings Bank in 1874. He explained what he meant to investors when the institution faced increasing pecuniary losses. "The Life, which was the money, was gone," says Douglass "and I found that I had been placed there with the hope that by 'some drugs, some charms, some *conjuration*, or some mighty magic, I would bring it back."[61] While Douglass was offended that he was being accused of thievery, we learn from his discussion of Sandy, that Douglass would have likely considered it an honor to be perceived as a sort of conjure doctor by members of the recently freed community had the circumstances been different. Stealing from other slaves laid in stark contradiction to the moral lessons on thievery that he had acquired from Sandy. It was believed that the latter was a justifiable act because it entailed taking that for which they had labored and their own bodies from those who seized their freedom.

Throughout his narratives and speeches Douglass also devoted a significant amount attention to his thoughts on Christianity. He touched upon his own spiritual awakening and how he, like other slaves, appropriated the religion to suit his own cultural and political needs. He offered criticisms of slave owners who claimed to be followers of Christ and he also discussed the limited access that most slaves had to Christian instruction. Sometime between 1831 and 1832 while he was living with Hugh and Sophia Auld, Douglass underwent a spiritual renewal. He was around twelve years old and his curiosity in the Bible and in Jesus Christ was sparked by a sermon he heard from Reverend Hanson, a local white Methodist minister who preached a gospel that promised equality to slaves and free persons so long as they sought protection in Christ. So intrigued by this message of parity, Douglass recalled retrieving discarded sheets of the Bible from the "filthy street gutters of Baltimore."[62] Douglass's efforts to collect soiled scriptures from the streets of Baltimore demonstrate their utter inaccessibility to the slave community.[63]

The commentary he provided on the lack of religious instruction for the slaves calls into question the notion that Christianity permeated the spiritual lives of the masses of slaves during the first half of the nineteenth century. When he addressed members of the Society of Friends in Bristol, England on August 25, 1846 Douglass deprecated the church and the clergy in the United States for caring more about the salvation of souls abroad then they did for their own population at home.[64] In Douglass's opinion herein lied the saddest paradox in the land of so-called civil and religious liberty. He wondered how the professors and ministers of Christianity could claim that they were part of the freest nation on the globe when the Bible Society neglected to share the Good Book with three million people.

Explaining how class often dictated who actually had the opportunity to hear Christian sermons he claimed in *My Bondage and My Freedom*: "The poor have the gospel preached to them, in this neighborhood, only when they are able to pay for it. The slaves having no money, get no gospel." It was not in the best interest of slaves to hear biblical messages that might incite feelings of equality or instill any desire to resist their oppression.[65] Douglass understood better than the master class that it was not possible to prevent the slaves from thinking about recalcitrant acts or to quell their

egalitarian desires. Nor did he think that the contemporary idea of plantation paternalism was truly reflective of slave life.[66]

Douglass was only about six years old when he first observed an act of
slave resistance. When he relocated to the Lloyd plantation he witnessed
several brutal physical attacks on the slaves. Because of their "shocking
nature" the floggings given to his Aunt Esther and a lady named Nelly were
the ones that stood out in his mind the most. It was from the latter incident
however that Douglass learned that slaves, despite their age, were not the
least bit docile when it came to protecting themselves. When Mr. Sevier,
Nelly's overseer, dragged her to a tree in front of her three children she put
up a strong fight despite the fact that she was no match for his strength.
Her fearless attitude was also exhibited in her children who assaulted the
overseer with stones.[67] The children's cries of *"Let my mammy go"—"Let
my mammy go"* could be heard over the overseer's curses. Nelly's children
ranged in age from seven to ten and were therefore old enough to understand the repercussions for their actions. However, at that crucial moment
of life or death, their natural instinct was to protect their primary caretaker
despite what might happen to them and few could have been more delighted
than Douglass that these little ones along with their mother would not lie
quietly. There have been no studies on the resistance of slave children yet
we find similar efforts from Harriet Jacob's children. It would of course be
interesting to find out if there were additional cases.[68]

The language that Douglass used to describe his previously mentioned
plan to escape with five other slaves in 1836 was imbued with radical revolutionary undertones. Appropriating the scriptures to their plight, Douglass
recalled the moment in which he contemplated the departure out of their
"Egypt." He and the others met under the guise of darkness every Sunday
and exchanged ideas about their concerns and expectations and how they
might confront any difficulty that they might encounter. Douglass felt that
"these meetings must have resembled, on a small scale, the meetings of
revolutionary conspirators, in their primary conditions." Their goal was
not to overthrow their masters but rather to escape from them. Nevertheless, the group believed that they had a right to their freedom "against every
obstacle—even against the lives of our enslavers." Douglass was around
eighteen years old at the time he was leading the plot. That he at this relatively young age considered striking down masters who presented themselves as a bulwark to their liberty is quite revolutionary.[69]

Douglass echoed these militant sentiments in an 1845 speech and again
in 1848. Shortly before Douglass's first narrative was published he gave an
address entitled *My Slave Experience in Maryland* at the Twelfth Annual
Convention of the American Anti-Slavery Society in New York. He conveyed to his northern audience that he was not a slave nor would he obedi-
ently surrender to being one ever again. Douglass warned that any master
who henceforth aimed to incarcerate him with chains "shall stand in as
much dread of me as I do him." While the master class could boast greater

numbers and were politically stronger than the slaves, Douglass informed them that if they continued to allow slavery to exist, they were doing so at their own risk.[70]

The Slaves' Right to Revolt was a speech that he delivered at the New England annual anti-slavery convention in 1848 in which he urged the north to relinquish their support for southern oppression and send the South a strong message that if they kept the slaves in shackles that they were doing so at their own expense and "peril!" Douglass said that there were great numbers of Nathaniel Turners in the South who would hero-ically surface if the north no longer backed the crimes of their southern neighbors. He wondered how Turner could be thought of as nothing less than brave when he sought to gain his freedom in a similar fashion to that of the founding fathers.[71]

Turner did not act according to the planter's ideas of plantation pater-nalism. Douglass dismissed the notion that slaves looked towards their masters for protection, direction, and benevolence in exchange for their unrequited labor. Peter Kolchin and Eugene Genovese are among those scholars who suggest that plantation paternalism was not only the corner-stone of the antebellum south but also worked to undermine the solidarity and African culture of slaves by inextricably linking them to *paternal*, lov-ing owners. However, Douglass tells us in *My Bondage and My Freedom* that the lessons offered by the slave priest craft on the duty of obedience to masters and the beneficial arrangement of slavery with its reciprocal benefits to both slaves and masters were simply untrue and often fell on deaf ears.[72]

Slavery was based on forced labor. Without Africans to plough the fields, drive the oxen, pick the cotton, labor in rice, tobacco, corn, wheat and indigo fields, retrieve and cook the food, do the blacksmithing and mechan-ical work, weave the garments, grind the grain, make the shoes, wait on the master class, raise their children, and engage in a host of other tasks the economic and social system would falter. Clearly the institution was not based on a relationship of *mutual* dependence and reciprocal benefits. The slave-owning class needed laborers much more than Africans needed mas-ters. As previously stated, Douglass took great comfort in knowing that, unlike those who were less fortunate, he enjoyed "the reciprocal duties and benefits of the relation" with a treasured loved one such as Betsy Bailey. It was through her, Uncle Lawson, Uncle Isaac Cooper, Uncle Toney, Uncle Harry, Uncle Abel, and Sandy Jenkins that he and the other slaves found protection, unconditional love, and guidance. Douglass disputed the idea that the relationships between slaves were undermined by their attachment to kind loving paternalistic owners.[73] He could not have imagined forsaking his fellow bondsmen and women for the slaveholder who "kind or cruel, is a slaveholder still—the every hour violator of the just and inalienable rights of man, and he is, therefore silently whetting the knife of vengeance for his own throat."[74]

Douglass found comfort in an anti-slavery Christianity that did not exclude or belittle the black race. He went against the grain in 1833 when he took it upon himself to establish a clandestine Sunday school for some of his fellow slaves with the purpose of teaching them to read. The meetings ceased to continue after his master Thomas Auld learned of them. Resilient in his efforts to help others attain some level of literacy Douglass organized and led another *hidden* Sunday school in 1835 while hired out to local farmer William Freeland. The initial meetings began during the summer months and were held secretly in various locations. Douglass and his congregation were eventually invited to conduct their services at the home of a free black man whose identity Douglass chose to conceal. At this second school Douglass instructed over forty scholars on how to read the Bible.[75] Throughout each of his narratives Douglass remained quite critical of other slaveholders who too sought religious justification for profits earned from slave labor. He was pleased, for example, to learn that when he left Covey's quarters in 1834 to live with William Freeland three miles outside of St. Michael's that the latter was not a man of the slaveholding religion. His experience with those who claimed to be devotedly committed to religious matters were most often the cruelest masters.[76]

In a figural sense Douglass functioned as a conjure doctor through his attempt to transform the minds and the practices of those who believed that slavery was right. His talisman of choice was the bible and his interpretation of the scriptures gave him the agency to morally attack slaveholders. Douglass believed that the bible was the most potent "medicine" for curing the ills of slavery. He thought that "Christianity proper" and the slaveholding religion were on the extreme opposite ends of the spectrum. He could not find any sound reason why the latter should even be called Christianity. Douglass felt that to do so was to comply with the most egregious lie possible. He devoted much of his public life to denouncing their "bad, corrupt, and wicked" religion in the same way a conjure doctor may have strove to rid their community of any maliciousness. He hoped to shake and rattle the very root and foundation of what was in his mind a false Christianity. He spoke of ministers who participated in the raising and selling and torturing of slaves. He accused church members of being "cradle plunders."[77]

Unlike most slaves, Douglass enjoyed the privilege of literacy. His ability to read the bible placed him in a position of power within the black community. He felt that if he could break down the legal barriers against teaching slaves to read that others would see that they too could transform, revise, and re-envision their social reality through this great book of life prescriptions.

The bible served as his "conjure book" through which he was able to refute everything slave masters stood for. How could they encourage the sacred institution of marriage on the one hand and deny it to slaves on the other Douglass wondered. He could not fathom why they advocated the importance and solidarity of their own family unit while scattering entire slave families apart from one another. Nor could he understand why they preached against the very crimes of which they were guilty. He accused them of erecting churches next to slave prisons and remained utterly repulsed by the idea that on any given Sunday one could find slave traders offering their blood-stained gold to the pulpit only to have their licentious actions cloaked "with the garb of Christianity."[78]

Douglass went so far as to condemn their religion as that of the devil "dressed in angels' robes, and hell presenting the semblance of paradise."[79] He denounced the popular scriptural interpretation that blacks as descendants of Ham were cursed to be slaves. He concluded that such an argument was without merit since there was a rising class of slaves who, like Douglass, were the offspring of their white master and slave mother.[80]

From the time Douglass first appeared on the lecture circuit up until his last years he continued to offer his opinions on what he felt was an insincere Christianity. The titles of a number of his speeches reflect his efforts to hold the slaveholding religion accountable for what he believed were their atrocious actions. From 1841 to 1846 he delivered the following address; "American Prejudice and American Religion," "The Church is the Bulwark of Slavery," "Southern Slavery and Northern Religion," "Irish Christians and Non-Fellowship with Man-Stealers," "Slavery Corrupts American Society and Religion," "The Bible Opposes Oppression, Fraud and Wrong," "Evangelical Man Stealers," and "Slavery Exists under the Eaves of the American Church."[81]

In 1849 he spoke on "Too Much Religion, Too Little Humanity." In 1852 he gave the well known "What to the Slave Is the Fourth of July?" speech in which he rebuked the doctors of divinity for participating in the slave trade. When he spoke about "Freedom in the West Indies" in 1858 he called his audience's attention to the susceptibility of the ministerial class to the "charms" of slavery. Douglass's use of the word "charms" to describe the malign forces of slavery parallels the African-American conjure doctor's understanding and acceptance of how one could fall victim to destructive forces. Again, Douglass believed that the most powerful talisman against this evil was the bible. His 1861 address "The American Apocalypse" given at the A.M.E. Zion Church in Rochester, New York blamed American Christianity for its hypocritical crimes against humanity. In 1870 he gave a speech entitled "A Reform Absolutely Complete" in which he expressed that he could in no way sympathize with any religion that discards its fellow citizens. Such sentiments were reiterated throughout all of his narratives.[82]

In response to questions of whether or not he was straying from the principles of Christianity when he offered critiques of the south's religion, Douglass relayed to the British public that though he was very much drawn to the message of Christ, he despised "the slaveholding, the woman-whipping, the mind darkening, the soul-destroying religion that exists in the southern states of America."[83] He stressed that he was in no way an infidel to Christianity but that he did "go for that infidelity which takes off chains, in preference to that religion which puts them on."[84]

The writings and speeches of Frederick Douglass call into question the claim that favorable articulations and invocations of Africa by newly freed blacks had much less to do with an actual understanding and familiarity of African culture than with a desire to be placed on equal footing with whites who could boast of having an esteemed history and legacy.[85] Douglass did strive to prove that blacks were not innately inferior to whites. However, his arguments were not created in an intellectual vacuum. He spoke from his experience as a slave on Colonel Lloyd's plantation when he compared the languages and dancing rituals of Africans and blacks in the United States. In addition to traveling to Africa he was an avid reader of contemporary histories and ethnographies. Douglass did recognize cultural boundaries that were imposed on the genre of the slave narrative as Stephen Butter-field and others have suggested.[86] Yet we learn from his rather detailed discussion of his grandmother, Christianity, paternalism, and resistance and his observations of the dialects spoken by slaves on the plantation, dancing rituals, work skills, manners, fictive kin relationships, conjuration and dreams that he, contrary to their conclusions, was able to maneuver around these boundaries.

Nathaniel P. Rogers was the editor of the anti-slavery journal *Herald of Freedom* and he provided one the most poignant accounts of Douglass's revolutionary character. Rogers reported on two speeches which Douglass gave in New Hampshire in 1844. As Douglass began to conclude the sec-ond speech Rogers witnessed in him a sort of

> volcanic outbreak of human nature long pent up in slavery and at last bursting its imprisonment. It was the storm of insurrection—and I could not but think, as he stalked to and fro on the platform, roused up like the Numidian Lion—how that terrible voice of his would ring through the pine glades of the South, in the day of her visitation—calling the insurgents to battle and striking terror to the hearts of the dismayed and despairing mastery. He reminded me of Toussaint among the plan-tations of Haiti . . . He was an insurgent slave taking hold on the right of speech, and charging on his tyrants the bondage of his race.[87]

Douglass's appreciation and unparalleled command of oratorical style can be largely attributed to the linguistic and cultural expressions he observed from his fellow slaves. Indeed, it was they who also helped to mold in him the spirit of Toussaint.

2 William Wells Brown
Subtle Whispers of Slave Culture, Pan-Africanism, and Insurgency

Often considered the first African-American historian, novelist and play-wright, William Wells Brown was one of the most prolific writers of the nineteenth century.[1] His discussion of African culture along with his ideas on the differences between his spiritual views and the religion esteemed by much of the master class provide us with another example of how an ex-slave who enjoyed the privilege of moving within highly visible political circles was able to offer insightful commentary on the counter-culture of blacks. Few, if any, have provided such detailed descriptions of slave-dancing rituals as Brown. His writings, like those of Douglass and the other authors of slave narratives treated throughout this project, call into question theories of plantation paternalism.

Though Brown pushed for integration early on in his abolitionist career and had a long-standing ideological feud with Henry Highland Garnet, he also exhibited a radical revolutionary outlook that has not received the attention it deserves. This chapter seeks to explore this aspect of Brown's life as well his observations and conclusions on the cultural attitudes of slaves and the master class by drawing on his speeches, narratives, works of fiction, and historical writings.

Brown discussed ceremonies of circular dance in two of his works. He first explored the subject in his final historical book which proved to be his longest monograph *The Rising Son; or, The Antecedents and Advancement of the Colored Race* (1874). The first part of this text as the title suggest lent close attention to what Brown believed were the African origins of the colored race. His chapter, "Civil and Religious Ceremonies," relied on some of the travel literature of the first half of the nineteenth century and includes a section on the dancing rituals of marriage and funeral rites among the Borers of Southern Africa. "When the appointed day for marriage has arrived," he writes, "the friends of the contracting parties assemble and form a circle; into this ring the bridegroom leads his lady-love." Towards the end of the ceremony the bride "breaks forth into joyful peals of *laughter,* in which all the company join, the musicians strike up a lively air, and the dance commences."[2]

Brown expressed that the funeral rituals of the Borers were just as fascinating:

> At the death of one of their number, the body is stripped, laid out upon the ground, and the friends of the deceased assemble, forming a circle around it, and commence howling like so many demons. They then march and counter-march around, with a subdued chant. After this, they hop around first on one foot, then on the other; stopping still, they cry at the top of their voices—"She's in Heaven, she's in Heaven!" Here they all fall flat upon the ground, and roll about for a few minutes, after which they simultaneously rise, throw up their hands, and run away yelling and *laughing*.[3]

Brown's reading of the contemporary travel literature led him to conclude that musical and dancing rituals were an important aspect in the everyday lives of African people. "With some of the tribes," he explained "instrumental music has been carried to a high point of culture."[4] While Brown referred to the religious practices of southern Africans as pagan, he was impressed with what was in his view a region of remarkable civilization. For him, what he termed "superstitious" practices and high culture were not irreconcilable. He believed that both were found throughout western and southern Africa.[5]

In Brown's last book *My Southern Home: Or, The South and Its People* he wrote about similar dancing rituals that he observed at a midnight camp meeting during his years in slavery. Consider his rather detailed account of one such gathering in St. Louis:

> The noise was hushed, and the assembled group assumed an attitude of respect. They made way for their queen and a short, black, old negress came upon the scene . . . and the crowd formed a *ring* around her . . . after a certain amount of gibberish and wild gesticulation . . . followed more gibberish and gesticulation, when the congregation joined hands, and began the wildest dance imaginable, keeping it up until the men and women sank to the ground from mere exhaustion.[6]

Brown knew that these practices were not uncommon "throughout the Southern states" where one could easily find "remnants of the old time Africans, who were stolen from their native land and sold in the Savannah, Mobile, and New Orleans markets, in defiance of all law." According to him, New Orleans was the center of such explicit activity:

> Congo Square takes its name, as is well known, from the Congo Negroes who used to perform their dance on its sward every Sunday. They were a curious people, and brought over with them this remnant of their African jungles. In Louisiana there were six different tribes of

negroes, named after the section of the country from which they came, and their representatives could be seen on the square, their teeth filed, and their cheeks still bearing tattoo marks.[7]

As many as three thousand onlookers would show up on any given Sunday to observe the "dusky dancers." The dancing was accompanied by banjoes, drums, and shakers and when the participants became aroused by the rhythmic synchronization of the instruments nothing could "faithfully portray the wild and frenzied motions" that caused many to *faint*. After exhaustion overcame one group another would enter the circle. Igobes, Fulani, Congolese, Mandingos, Kormantins were some of the groups involved in the ceremonies. "These dances," Brown declared, "were kept up until within the memory of men still living, and many who believe in them and who would gladly revive them, may be found in every state in the Union."[8] Brown provides an insightful window into the cultural ethos of freed peoples who were more than willing to hold on to African values fifteen years after slavery ended.

Brown had the chance to witness an extraordinary ring shout at a Revival in Nashville Tennessee. He recalled:

> The church was already filled, when the minister had taken his text. As the speaker warmed up in his subject, the Sisters began to swing their heads and reel to and fro, and eventually began a shout. Soon, five or six were fairly at it, which threw the house into a buzz. Seats were soon vacated near the shouters, to give them more room, because the women did not wish to have their hats smashed by the *frenzied* Sisters. As a woman sprung up in her seat, throwing up her long arms, with a loud scream the lady on the adjoining seat quickly left, and did not stop till she got to a safe distance.[9]

Brown's scholarly and literary efforts gave him the space to seriously explore similar dancing ceremonies on both sides of the Atlantic. By the time *My Southern Home* was printed, seven years had passed since Brown dealt with African dance in *The Rising Son*. For him the similarities would have been obvious. If Brown was at all ashamed of these practices it did not prevent him from writing about them in works which sought in some way to dispute contemporary notions of black inferiority.[10] Moreover, his attempt to establish cultural links between slaves and their African predecessors is quite impressive for one who, like Frederick Douglass, lacked a formal education.

Brown understood how these cultural connections could also be found in the slaves' socio-religious expression of conjuration. His personal feelings on the matter were ambiguous. He questioned the authenticity of self-proclaimed soothsayers, yet frequented one believed to be versed in the ways of conjuration and discussed conjuration in five of his published works. In

Narrative of William W. Brown (1847) Brown revealed that, just prior to his escape from slavery in St. Louis, he solicited the help of Uncle Frank, a highly regarded local conjure doctor who maintained a large black and white clientele.[11] While the number of times Brown went to Uncle Frank is unknown, he did admit that "whether the old man was a prophet, or the son of a prophet, I cannot say; but there is one thing certain, many of his predictions were verified." Uncle Frank was described as a tall gentleman in his seventies with a slim build who was known to have a number of women patrons. "Whether true or not," Brown related "he had the *name*, and that is about half of what one needs in this gullible age." Brown's suggestion that those who believed in Uncle Frank's gift were naïve is not his definitive stance on the matter. He was quite impressed by Uncle Frank's apparent success and, despite his claim to be "no believer in soothsaying," he noted Uncle Frank's prophetic accuracy that followed his "looking into a gourd, filled with water." That Brown conferred with Uncle Frank before his perilous attempt to run away suggests that he did not take the elder's profession lightly.[12]

Brown briefly mentioned another conjure doctor who was versed in the ways of fortune-telling in his historical novel *Clotel: or, The President's Daughter* (1853).[13] Considered the first work of fiction by an African-American, this book has received a fair amount of attention from literary critics. It is rather well known that *Clotel* is about the challenges that confront Currer, a mulatto slave from Virginia, and her quadroon daughters Clotel and Athesa. Scholars have generally offered their interpretations of the story's main plot, which revolves around the interracial relationship between Clotel and her master, Horatio Green.[14]

The chapter "A Night in the Parson's Kitchen" describes what life was like for Currer after she was sold to the Reverend John Peck, a Methodist preacher from Mississippi. Currer was one of five domestic servants for Peck. One Sam, originally of Kentucky, was employed as the head house slave. Through Sam's character, Brown touches upon the tensions that existed between darker slaves and their mulatto counterparts and the ability of domestic servants to remain connected to the African culture of the greater slave community. Unlike most slaves, Sam enjoyed the advantage of being able to read. While this privilege set him apart from the other slaves he was forced to confront the racial hardships that came along with having the darkest complexion among his peers. Quite ashamed of this, Sam claimed to have had white blood running through his veins and was constantly seeking to alter his appearance to prove it. Despite Sam's self deprecation, he embraced conjuration as it related to fortune-telling.

At one of Peck's parties which was attended by several female maid servants of neighboring estates, Sam, in an attempt to court one of the ladies, declared "I jist bin had my fortune told last Sunday night . . . Aunt Winny told me I is to hab de prettiest yaller gal in town, and dat I is to be free." Aunt Winny calls to mind the real life Uncle Frank described in Brown's narrative. Uncle Frank told Brown on the eve of his escape that he too should be free.[15] Though Brown did not devote much attention to the conjuring culture of slaves in *Clotele*, Sam's consultation with Aunt Winny serves as valuable commentary on the influence of African cultural values even on those slaves who lived in the big house and were in that sense close to the master class.

Brown discussed the conjuring culture of slaves again in his play *The Escape; Or, A Leap For Freedom* (1858) which was the first dramatic piece published by an African-American. For this work Brown drew heavily on his own experiences while living in the South and included actual people with who he came into contact.[16] The plot revolved around a forced romantic relationship between slave owner Dr. Gaines and his mulatto slave Melinda. When Dr. Gaines told Melinda that she was not to have any relationship outside of theirs and that it was in his power to do whatever he pleased to her she warned him that if he in any way sought to cause her demise she would put a curse on him:

> Sir, let me warn you that if you compass my ruin, a woman's bitterest curse will be laid upon your head, with all the crushing, withering weight that my soul can impart to it; a curse that shall cling to you throughout the remainder of your wretched life; a curse that shall haunt you like a spectre in your dreams by night, and attend upon you by day; a curse, too, that shall embody itself in the ghastly form of the woman whose chastity you will have outraged.[17]

Brown claimed that at the time he wrote the play Melinda was still living in Canada.[18]

Brown continued to explore the conjuring culture of slaves through his treatment of Nat Turner in his seminal historical book *The Black Man, His Antecedents, His Genius, and His Achievements* (1863).[19] Brown sought to accomplish two things in writing this volume. First, he wanted to demonstrate that "the negro has that intellectual genius which God has planted in the mind of man, that distinguishes him from the rest of creation." Second, he hoped to fill a void in nineteenth-century scholarship by highlighting the accomplishments of African-Americans who by the very nature of their lot overcame what seemed to be insurmountable odds.[20]

Brown's account of Turner is the longest of the fifty-three biographical sketches included in the volume.[21] In the introduction Brown explained that given Turner's early upbringing around the superstitious beliefs found within the slave quarters along with his mother instilling in him that he was born to be a prophet that would help emancipate his race, it should come as no surprise that such principles were manifested in him in his adult life. Brown's Nat Turner "unlike most of those born under the influence of slavery" did not fully embrace the African cultural influences of "conjuring, fortune-telling, or dreams" until he claimed to have received a vision from

God during the time he remained in the woods as an escapee for thirty days. Turner believed he was being called upon to return from the wilderness and lead the slaves in battle against their masters.[22]

Following his detailed account of Turner's 1831 unsuccessful rebellion, Brown informed the reader of the insurgent's last words, "bury my axe with me." Brown averred that Turner "religiously believed that in the next world the blacks would have a contest with the whites, and that he would need his axe." Turner was a hero in Brown's eyes and he seems to have had a sincere appreciation for Turner's African sensibility as it related to his prophecies and views of the afterlife.[23]

Brown also warned the southern people that if they did not want history to repeat itself they would be wise to learn a lesson from Turner's uprising and other acts of insubordination by the slave community. Brown argued that the non-slave-holding states would no longer view the slaves' fight for freedom with the same contempt as they had thirty years previously during the Turner insurrection. "If the oppressor is struck down in the contest," he reasoned "his fall will be a just one, and all the world will applaud the act." He believed that it was just a matter of time before another Nat Turner would emerge from the South.[24]

As previously noted, Brown sought to establish African cultural origins for blacks in *The Rising Son* (1873). Included in his discussion is an examination of African conjure doctors, about whom he writes:

> One of the most influential and important classes in every African community is the deybo, a set of professional men who combine the medical and priestly office in the same person. They attend the sick and administer medicines, which usually consist of decoctions of herbs or roots, and external applications. A doctor is expected to give his undivided attention to one patient at a time, and is paid only in case of successful treatment.[25]

According to Brown, it was not uncommon for the doctor to provide the family with some of his hair which was removed from his head at the time he was officially inducted into the priestly and medical office. This exchange served as a security to ensure that the requested services were rendered, as it was believed that without this bundle of hair the practitioner was devoid of his skill.[26]

Brown touched upon the African conjure doctor's ability to not only heal but to also inflict harm through malign forces. He asserted that in order to hold this office one was required to journey through a two-year rite of passage under the tutelage of one who was an esteemed member of the fraternity. This class of individuals was revered and feared. It was believed that they could "raise the dead, cast out devils, and do all manner of things that other people are incapable of doing." [27]

The Rising Son offered a pan-African view by exploring regions throughout the African Diaspora. Drawing from James M. Phillippo's *Jamaica,*

Past and Present (1843), Brown considered the various ethnic groups that contributed to the island's population and provided a detailed account of their religious experiences.[28] He asserted that "many of the original stock of slaves had been imported from amongst the Mandingoes, and Foulahs, from the banks of the Senegal, the Gambia, and the Rio Grande . . . and from the Congoes of Upper and Lower Guinea."[29] Brown explained that the Jamaican conjure doctor practiced the African-influenced religious system known as obeism which through the use of charms sought to avenge injuries, serve as protection against theft and murder, and aid one in winning a particular love interest. He also indicated that dreams and visions were an important aspect of their spiritual beliefs.[30]

Brown's last and most extensive discussion of the African-American conjure doctor is found in *My Southern Home* (1880). Since this was his last book, published fifteen years after slavery had ended, it is not beyond reason to conclude that he felt less pressure to allow stereotypical notions of black cultural inferiority enter his text. Here, he reintroduces the reader to Uncle Frank who was also mentioned in his narrative.[31]

It was well known throughout Brown's St. Louis community that a Mrs. McWilliams won a lawsuit by consulting Uncle Frank. Unsure of which lawyers she should choose to represent her, she, like Brown and many others, sought advice from the senior fortuneteller. Uncle Frank stared at her for awhile and said "missis, you's got your mind on two lawyers,—a big man and a little man. Ef you takes de big man you loses de case, ef you takes de little man, you wins de case." Mrs. McWilliams was indeed considering two lawyers. "So, taking the old negro's advice, she obtained the services of John F. Darby, and gained the suit."[32]

Dinkie was the conjure doctor that received the most attention in *My Southern Home* and he and Brown enjoyed a close friendship in St. Louis. Dinkie was born in Africa and it was believed that he was the progeny of royal lineage. Known for wearing a snake skin around his neck and carrying a stiff frog and dried lizard in his pocket Dinkie, like Uncle Frank, was respected by both blacks and whites. Brown tells us that he was the best at his craft in their section of St. Louis.[33] Dinkie often proved to be too much to handle for the local overseers and no one could recall an instance in which he was summoned to do any strenuous work. Whites often "tipped their hats to the old one-eyed Negro," and while other slaves were frequently harassed by the patrollers Dinkie was left alone. On one occasion Brown queried a gentleman on why people feared Dinkie. The man's response is an example of the slaves' desire to conceal their true opinions about slave culture. The man initially indicated that he was not at all afraid of the old conjurer. "He then took a look around and behind," writes Brown, "as if he feared some one would hear what he was saying, and then continued: 'Dinkie's got de power, ser; he knows things seen and unseen, an' dat's what makes him his own massa."[34]

While Brown and the other slaves looked favorably upon persons such as Dinkie, Brown thought it "quite extraordinary that well-educated men and women" relied on the oracle.[35] One white lady who visited the Poplar Farm requesting Dinkie's intuitive insights was Martha Lemmy. There was no need for her to inform Dinkie of why she had come, for he already knew the visit was regarding a particular love interest. Dinkie read her palm and assured her that Mr. Scott, a wealthy landowner, would ask for her hand in marriage as long as she held on to the goopher powder that Dinkie had given her.[36] Other whites also believed Dinkie had "de power." Brown tells of the time when a Mr. Sarpee visited the Poplar farm and fell victim to the stench of a skunk while out on hunting excursion. Again, Dinkie prescribed goopher and all were convinced that the remedy worked.[37] Soil from deep beneath the earth served as a key ingredient for the concoction and slaves often relied on dirt from the graveyards when assembling goopher powders.[38]

Dinkie was not the only oracle that whites consulted. Brown tells us of the time when Mr. Lemmy, Martha's husband, visited "old Betty, the blind fortuneteller" to find out which horses were going to win the races. She was correct to suggest that he gamble on the gray mare, the likely underdog. Mr. Lemmy never bet on a horse without consulting old Betty and he like many of the local blacks also believed that spirits walked among the living.[39] For Brown, cultural connections and influences were worthy of analysis. He concluded that such beliefs among whites in St. Louis "was the result of their close connection with the blacks." The servants shared their stories with the young children in the nurseries who continued to absorb black culture from the field hands as they grew older. These same influences were responsible for Brown's appreciation for slave culture. [40]

Also included in the cultural memory of slaves was the belief that there existed certain *signs* or omens that symbolically represented things to come. These *signs* often functioned as sort of roadmap for the decisions one should make. Brown described how some South Carolinian slaves interpreted *signs* on the eve of their emancipation. When they convened on a stormy night and heard a sound come from a banjo hanging up on the wall they interpreted it as a sign from "de angles" indicating that freedom would soon be theirs:

> Dou did promise dat one of dy angels should come an' give us de sign, an' shore 'nuff de sign did come. We's grateful, O, we's grateful, O, Lord, send dy angel once moe to give dat sweet sound.[41]

This was followed by another shriek from the banjo accompanied by lightning and thunder. They then rose to their feet and began to shout and sing a spiritual whose chorus was "send them angles down."[42] Brown could not convince the group that the sound could only be attributed to the strong wind. "Oh, no ser," declared Uncle Ben, "dat come fum de angles. We been specken it all de time. We know the angles struck the strings of de banjo."[43]

Though Brown appeared to be a nonbeliever, he admitted that "all sorts of stories were soon introduced to prove that angelic visits were common, especially to those who were fortunate enough to carry 'de witness.'"[44] Uncle Ben confessed that he was visited by "de Lord" the previous night in his sleep. Then there was the old slave who announced that she knew something good was bound to happen when the angels had lifted her out of her bed three times the night before. Someone else recalled experiencing the good omen of dropping a fork that "stuck up in de floo." Another revealed that "De mule kicked at me three times dis mornin' an' he never did dat afore in his life an' I knowed good luck would come fum dat." There was also Uncle Ben's wife who felt that something good was going to happen after she saw a rabbit run across her path.[45]

While Brown may not have always embraced the African culture to which he gave considerable attention, he understood that it served as the primary source for the values and ideas of the great majority of slaves.[46] He included a discussion of slave culture in most of his writings. Brown was, in addition, the only nineteenth-century author to explore African culture in works of fiction, history, drama, and biography.

As shown, at times he did subscribe to the popular contemporary notions that African culture was not on par with the culture of whites. By the same token there were a number of instances in which Brown expressed favorable sentiments on the widespread African cultural influences found within the slave quarters. That he may not have been able to personally resolve his feelings on African culture, in part because of the negative attitudes towards the culture, does not undermine the valuable contributions he made to the understanding of slave life.

Brown was not nearly as critical of the persistence of African values in the slave community as he was of what he termed the "slaveholders' Christianity." To be certain, Brown proudly considered himself a follower of Christ. Nevertheless, he illustrated how his personal experiences as a slave in St. Louis informed his castigation of those who he thought professed to be Christians in name only and perpetuated the spirit of inequality intrinsic to American slavery. Such a paradox made little sense to Brown and it was a constant theme throughout his writings and speeches.[47]

Recalling the time when he worked as a waiter on board the *Enterprise*, a merchant vessel that traversed the upper Mississippi River near St. Louis, Brown explained how he often dreamt of breaking the chains of slavery by crossing the Canadian border. For Brown, no other place superseded the callousness of Missouri slave life. Some of his more memorable atrocities included the time a high-ranking officer in the U.S. armed forces beat a woman to death, or few could forget the occasion when Francis McIntosh, a free black passing through from Pittsburg, was snatched from a vessel and set ablaze.[48]

Just prior to his employment on the *Enterprise* Brown was the victim of severe physical assaults. These occurred during the time he was hired out as a press operator and messenger for the *St. Louis Times.* While returning from running an errand to the publishing office of the *Missouri Republican* a number of young boys, the sons of slave owners, assaulted him. Adding insult to injury, one of the youth's fathers, Samuel McKinney, caned Brown in retaliation for the serious wounds inflicted on his son during the scuffle. Unable to walk for over a month, Brown could not hold his job at the *St. Louis Times* and promises of a better life in Canada echoed like soothing music to his ears.[49]

Brown could not bear the thought of leaving behind his family who remained in captivity. Convincing his mother to accompany him on the journey was no easy task—as she too did not want to part from her loved ones. Yet Brown's unrelenting appeals for his mother's change of heart eventually worked and together with the North Star as their guide they set sail on a skiff towards Illinois.[50]

Reflecting on the first few days of the journey Brown poignantly described some of his innermost feelings: "When I thought of slavery with its Democratic whips—its Republican chains—its evangelical blood hounds, and its religious slave-holders—when I thought of all this paraphernalia of American Democracy and Religion behind me, and the prospect of liberty before me, I was encouraged to press forward, my heart was strengthened, and I forgot that I was tired or hungry."[51]

Unfortunately for Brown and his mother three slave catchers apprehended them on the eleventh day of their trek about one hundred and fifty miles outside of St. Louis. "The man who but a few hours before had bound my hands together with a strong cord," explained Brown, "read a chapter from the Bible, and then offered up prayer, just as though God sanctioned the act he had just committed upon a poor panting, fugitive slave. The next morning, a blacksmith came in, and put a pair of handcuffs on me, and we started on our journey back to the land of whips, chains, and *Bibles.*"[52]

Brown felt that slaveholders were the worst kind of cowards who hid behind one of their most treasured allies—the church. "A more praying, preaching, psalm-singing people," he writes, "cannot be found than the slaveholders at the south." He added "the religion of the south is referred to every day, to prove that slaveholders are good, pious men. But with all their pretensions, and all the aid which they get from the northern church, they cannot succeed in deceiving the Christian portion of the world." Brown was convinced that "their child-robbing, man-stealing, woman-whipping, chain-forging, marriage-destroying, slave-manufacturing, man-slaying religion, will not be received as genuine."[53]

From a young age Brown rejected the religious culture of the master class and he often dreaded the approach of the Sabbath. Brown sadly recalled the events of a particular Sunday that had left him emotionally shaken. After witnessing D. D. Page, a highly regarded Baptist minister, severely injure his slaves he wondered how slaveholders could actually consider themselves Christians "while robbing three million of their countrymen of their liberties."[54]

Brown was disappointed when his master "got religion" and invited a preacher to deliver nightly sermons just to the slaves so that they would absorb the masters' biblical justifications for slavery. Slaves were instructed never to strike a white man; that God ordained them to be slaves; and that they were to humbly surrender to their masters' physical punishments. For the last lesson masters would quote the scripture that says, "He that knoweth his master's will, and doeth it not, shall be beaten with many stripes."[55] When slave owners, including everyone "from the doctor of divinity down to the most humble lay member in the church," sought to impress a potential buyer they would often say the slave had religion meaning that he or she did not stray from these cardinal principles of unconditional servility.

The writings of Brown provide us with another example of how slaves dismissed a religion which they believed failed to live up to its doctrinal creed. When many expressed their allegiance to the Christian faith or claimed to have "had religion" they did not feel that they were acting in accordance with the master class's biblical appropriation of the obedient servant doctrine. Rather they were fashioning their own ideas about what Christianity meant to them. To embrace their masters' religion would mean that they were sanctioning the wrongs that were being committed against them.[56]

When Brown later addressed the Pennsylvania Anti-Slavery Society on October 23, 1854 he underscored his strong feelings against the southern slave trade and reiterated his view on the religious practices of slaveholders. He assailed the various Christian denominations that were actively participating in the trade and challenged his audience to pass through southern markets as he had done while hired out to slave trader James Walker. There they would "see Methodist carting Methodist to the market and selling him, Baptist whipping Baptist, and Presbyterian purchasing Presbyterian, and Episcopalian tying chains upon the limbs of Episcopalians and then talk about national character and honor!"[57]

As Brown's narratives and speeches have made clear, there was a wide gap between the slave owners' ideas about the religious attitudes that slaves should possess and the degree to which they actually embraced the doctrine of unwavering obedience. Slaves were not simply pawns in a game of paternalistic chess.[58] Brown, like Douglass, rejected the idea that slave owners were kind-loving paternal masters who typically cared about the well-being of their slaves. "The fact that a slaveholder feeds his slaves better, clothes them better, than another," he argued "does not alter the case; he is a slaveholder."[59]

Brown offered a similar critique of paternalism through his character Jerome, Clotelle's love interest, in his novel *Clotelle*. In response to one slaveholder's assertion that he always treated his slaves well Jerome explained their right to be free . . . is taken from them, and they have no security for their comfort, but the humanity and generosity of men, who have been trained to regard them not as brethren, but as mere property. Humanity and generosity are, at best, but poor guaranties for the protection of those who cannot assert their rights, and over whom law throws no protection.[60]

Jerome was determined never to let a white man flog him. When his master Mr. Wilson grabbed his throat Jerome retaliated by knocking him down and fled to the nearby woods.[61] When he was later apprehended and questioned about rumors of a slave conspiracy Jerome belligerently told his masters that if he was aware of a plot to revolt he would not reveal it. Even though Jerome was facing death for his crime of insolence and was offered a lesser sentence if he could provide any information regarding the conspiracy, he remained silent on the matter. He said that because slaves had no right to their own bodies, their spouses, or their children that the full human experiences was denied to them. Jerome was not afraid to admit that he affirmed the slaves' desire to overthrow the power structure:

> If I mistake not, the day will come when the negro will learn that he can get his freedom by fighting for it; and should that time arrive, the whites will be sorry that they have hated us so shamefully. I am free to say that, could I live my life over again, I would use all the energies which God has given me to get up an insurrection.[62]

All who were present were "startled and amazed at the intelligence with which this descendant of Africa spoke." He was regarded as a very dangerous slave who must have been spoiled by some book learning.[63]

In his narrative Brown spoke quite fondly of Randall, another fellow bondsmen in Missouri who refused to let any overseer whip him. Brown was so impressed with Randall's courage that he devoted an entire chapter to him. Few on the plantation escaped the lash. This was not the case with Randall. The physically superior and strong-willed slave could often be heard saying that he would die before succumbing to a flogging. Brown could not recall an instance in which Randall was not true to his word. The resident overseer was determined to make an example out of Randall and commanded three men to assist in subduing him. Randall was victorious against the assailants until one fired a pistol at him. Clearly Brown was familiar with and appreciative of recalcitrant slaves. He respected Randall's determination to defy any attempts to cause him harm. However he and the other slaves on the plantation were probably deeply affected when Randall was given a hundred lashes and forced to labor with a ball and chain attached to his leg after he was debilitated from the gun shout wound.[64] It is highly likely that both Randall and the resilient conjure doctor Dinkie who Brown befriended in St. Louis and discusses in *My Southern Home* provided at least some of the inspiration for the literary figure Jerome in *Clotelle*. Moreover, Brown would have certainly been familiar with Frederick Douglass's narratives and might have also used Douglass's lengthy discussion of *root* specialist Sandy Jenkins as literary models to explore the conjurer doctor motif in his own works.

Clotelle also allowed Brown to explore the resistance of slave children. When a slave trader came to seize Isabella, Clotelle's mother, the young Clotelle retrieved a walking stick and threatened "if you bad people touch my mother, I will strike you." Brown narrates:

> They looked at the child with astonishment; and her extreme youth, wonderful beauty, and uncommon courage, seemed for a moment to shake their purpose. The manner and language of this child were alike beyond their years, and under other circumstances would have gained for the approbation of those present.[65]

This passage calls to mind Douglass's observation of child resistance discussed in chapter one. Implicit in both authors' accounts was their consensus that Africans were not innately driven to be slaves as apologists for slavery had argued.[66] As Clotelle grew into adulthood she did not abandon her desire to unselfishly assist her loved ones. It was she who designed the scheme for Jerome's successful escape from prison. During a visit to his holding cell Clotelle suggested that they switch clothes giving Jerome the opportunity to slip by the unsuspecting jailer.[67]

Brown also challenged the paternalist notion of dependence in *The Black Man*. He argued that slaves were the main producers of southern agriculture and ipso facto the primary reason that the Northern colonies and Europe were able to reap significant pecuniary benefits from cotton, sugar, and rice worked by slaves. Thus, for Brown it was the slaveholding class who depended on the slaves and not vice versa:

> "What shall be done with the slaves if they are freed?" You had better ask, "What shall we do with the slaveholders if the slaves are freed?" The slave has shown himself better fitted to take care of himself than the slaveholder. He is the bone and sinew of the south; he is the producer, while the master is nothing but a consumer, and a very poor consumer at that. The slave is the producer, and he alone can be relied upon . . . the slaves can take care of themselves.[68]

Brown's main purpose here was to argue against those members of the American Colonization Society (ACS) who were pushing for the forced expatriation of slaves. He sought to demonstrate that it was not in the best interest of anyone, especially the planter class, to remove the main labor source from the South.

Though Brown eschewed the design of the ACS, he often exhibited a pan-African outlook in his writings and organizing efforts and, like many of his contemporaries following the enactment of the Fugitive Slave Law of 1850, eventually pushed for voluntary emigration to Haiti.[69] Insurgents such as Nat Turner and Toussaint L'Ouverture emerged as protagonists throughout Brown's works. His ambiguity on radical revolutionary modes of slave resistance can be attributed in part to his visible position as a Garrisonian on the one hand and his desire to provide an honest account of his observations and true feelings of slave life on the other. In order to fully understand Brown's feelings on slave resistance it is necessary to consider his writings as a whole. Through this approach we can unearth Brown's broad understanding of the slaves' refusal to accept the order of things.

In *The Black Man* Brown revisited the subject of insurgency by chronicling the lives of blacks throughout the African Diaspora who exhibited revolutionary ideas and actions. As already noted, Nat Turner received the most attention and Brown made it a point to mention that he, like several of the other people profiled in the text, was "of unmixed African descent."[70] Among those who received similar praise for what Brown believed were their heroic exploits included Madison Washington, Placido, Toussaint L'Ouverture, Joseph Cinque, and Phillis Wheatley. The common thread that linked all of them with the likes of Nat Turner was their determination to strike a blow at slavery without fear or reservation.

Brown applauded Madison Washington, who was also "born of African parentage," for his successful 1841 uprising on board the *Creole,* a Virginia slave trading vessel that supplied the New Orleans market. After successfully escaping to Canada, Washington had decided to return to Virginia, the place of his birth place, with the hope of inciting a slave insurrection to free his wife and others who were still held in bondage. He was quickly discovered and sold to a slave trader who placed him with his other cargo destined for the New Orleans market. Washington's fate seemed bleak. Still, his rebellious spirit remained unbroken. On the ninth day of the journey the ship encountered rough seas leaving a good number of the slaves sick. Realizing that the crew let its guard down because they felt less threatened by their ill cargo, Washington realized that it was the opportune time to strike. He along with the others he recruited seized their freedom by taking down their captors and piloting the vessel to Nassau, New Providence.[71]

Not all were as successful as Washington. Nevertheless, in the eyes of Brown their efforts were no less courageous. Placido, a former Cuban slave known for his poignant poetry, was one such hero. He was brought to the sugar colony directly from Africa. After he received his freedom in 1842 Placido endeavored to liberate others. He began to write verses that were put to music with the hope of inspiring slaves to take their freedom. Placido eventually devised an insurrection that he would lead. The plot failed and he was sentenced to death. Brown may have taken a particular interest in Placido because of the Afro-Cuban's mission to promote an anti-slavery gospel through song. Brown had sought to do the same thing with his publication *The Anti-Slavery Harp: A Collection of Songs for Anti-Slavery Meetings* (1848).[72]

Brown, like David Walker and Henry Highland Garnet, held Toussaint L'Ouverture and his military expertise in leading the Haitian slave rebellion against the French in high regard. Because Toussaint was "the grandson of the King of Ardra, one of the most powerful and wealthy monarchs on the west coast of Africa," it made sense to Brown that he would eventually lead his people to freedom and establish a new government in Santo Domingo. Brown drew comparisons between him and George Washington who also established a government in the new world.[73] As leaders of oppressed people both men had a formidable foe with which to contend. The key difference, Brown stressed, was that Toussaint integrated ideas of liberty for all and outlawed the slave trade in his constitution while Washington sanctioned the existence of slavery and the slave trade in his. Brown was convinced that "when impartial history shall do justice to the St. Domingo revolution, the name of Toussaint L'Overture will be placed high upon the roll of fame."[74]

In his account of Joseph Cinque, leader of the 1839 ship rebellion on board the *Amistad*, Brown implied once again that the great genius of the mutineer could largely be attributed to him being "a native of Africa, and one of the finest specimens of his race ever seen in this country."[75] Brown viewed Phillis Wheatley in a similar light. He believed that through her poetry this treasured "daughter of Africa had an opportunity of developing the genius that God had given her, and of showing to the world the great wrong done to her race."[76]

Brown included a number of other nineteenth-century blacks who rose to some level of prominence. Perhaps the most fascinating is that of Henry Highland Garnet. It is especially intriguing in light of the ideological controversies between Garnet and Brown. Brown was one of the members of the American Anti-Slavery Society in attendance at the 1843 National Convention of Colored citizens in Buffalo, New York who rejected the adoption of Garnet's radical call to violence in his *Address to the Slaves of the United States of America*.[77]

Remaining true to Garrisonian principles, Brown also differed with Garnet on whether or not partisan politics should play a role in the abolitionist cause. Garnet was a strong advocate and recruiter for the Liberty party while Brown strove to promote moral suasion. When the Liberty party held their national convention in Buffalo two weeks following the National Convention of Colored Citizens, Brown, in an article published in the *National Anti-Slavery Standard*, refuted Garnet's claim that the resolution of the party "was adopted, with but two opposing votes." Brown explained that "Mr. Garnet knew, as did every member of that convention, that there were more than two that voted against the resolution adopting the views of the liberty party." Brown felt that Garnet committed a grave disservice to the anti-slavery movement by failing to acknowledge the many delegates present who were not constituents of the Liberty party. "When I see such quibbling, by such men as Henry Highland Garnet," he writes "it makes me tremble for the fate of the slave at the hands of political parties."[78]

This was not the last of their controversy. The feud was reignited sixteen years later when Brown spoke out against the emigration policies of the American Colonization Society and the African Civilization Society at "a Convention of the Colored Citizens" held in Boston on May, 3 1859. Brown felt that these organizations erroneously assumed that blacks could not integrate into American society. He also elaborated on what he considered to be the African Civilization Society's demeaning tendency to beg for support. Garnet, then president of the Society, responded to Brown's accusations by charging Brown with begging in Great Britain and in America. Brown denied such claims and dared Garnet "to name the time and place where he had heard me 'crave a collection to pay expenses.'" Brown invited Garnet to Boston to discuss the matter. There is no evidence that Garnet accepted the challenge.[79]

These public disagreements did not preclude Brown from writing an extensive treatment of Garnet in *The Black Man* and is reflective of his philosophical growth. Brown, as he had done with others, mentioned Garnet's African heritage and remarked that he was the son of an African chief. He praised Garnet for acquiring "the reputation of a courteous and accomplished man, an able and eloquent debater, and a good writer" at Oneida Institute in New York. Brown also wrote quite favorably of Garnet's moral character and credited him with being an exceptional orator. He even noted the persuasive impact of Garnet's 1843 *Address to the Slaves* despite his earlier critique of the lecture. "None but those who heard the speech" he wrote "have the slightest idea of the tremendous influence which he exercised over the assembly."[80]

To support his claim that Garnet was a proficient author, Brown included a lengthy excerpt of his writings that reflected Garnet's pan-African outlook. In one section Garnet writes "if I might apostrophize that bleeding country, I would say, O Africa, thou hast bled, freely bled, at every pore. Thy sorrow has been mocked, and thy grief has not been heeded. Thy children are scattered over the whole earth, and the great nations have been enriched by them."[81] Brown seems to have appreciated the endeavors of Garnet almost in the same way he valued the exploits of Turner, Toussaint, and other radicals or revolutionaries.

Four years after *The Black Man* was published Brown continued his treatment of black insurgents in *The Negro in the American Rebellion* (1867). The crux of the text, which details the role that black soldiers played in the Civil War, is preceded by a discussion of black participation in the American Revolution and the War of 1812 and biographical sketches of Denmark Vesey, Nat Turner, and Madison Washington that are similar to those found in *The Black Man*. He also included an account of John Brown's raid at Harper's Ferry and the slave revolt on board the *Creole*.

Brown revisited the theme of resistance in *The Rising Son* (1874). Here he included another lengthy treatment on Haiti lending special attention to Toussaint and Dessalines. This text contains what is probably the first scholarly discussion on slave resistance in the United States in a chapter entitled "Colored Insurrections in The Colonies." In this section he touched upon a series of revolts and conspiracies spanning from the New York Slave rebellion of 1712 to Gabriel Prosser's 1830 plot in Virginia. Brown explored the acts of Denmark Vesey and Nat Turner more closely in his chapter "Discontent and Insurrection." Ever the student of ship rebellions Brown also felt that it was necessary to write another account of the schooner *Amistad* and the brig *Creole* in his chapter "Heroism At Sea."[82]

Throughout his life Brown was devoted to a moral anti-slavery movement that did not lack radical or cultural qualities. His careful attention to slave culture is exhibited throughout each of his texts. His insightful discussion of circular dance in Africa along with his commentary on the ring shout in St. Louis, New Orleans and Nashville is unparalleled by a black abolitionist. He realized that Uncle Frank, Dinkie, Old Betty, and other conjure doctors with whom he was familiar served an important function in the slave community. He understood that these wise elders were keepers of an intricate African past and they were not unlike the African deybo doctor who is described in *The Rising Son*. Like Frederick Douglass he sought to quiet stereotypes of black inferiority.

Brown was a Pan-Africanist at heart who praised the acts of black insurgents throughout the African Diaspora and remained sharply critical of the slaveholders' religion and ideas of plantation paternalism. He wrote not only from the position of an intellectual but, more importantly, from the ranks of the slave. Reflecting on the writer's purpose in life, Brown, himself ever the consummate author, must have had the aims of his recently freed fellow bondsmen and women in mind when he wrote in *My Southern Home*:

> Indeed, authors possess the most gifted and fertile minds who combine all the graces of style with rare, fascinating powers of language, eloquence, wit, humor, pathos, genius and learning. And to draw knowledge from such sources should be one of the highest aims of man.[83]

None more than the slave class to whom literacy wad denied for so long could empathize with these sentiments. It was their unconditional emancipation that remained the focus of Brown's life and through his work we learn that he was among the most formidable cultural critics of slave life.

3 "Moses Is Got De Charm"
Harriet Tubman's Mosaic Persona

In the African-American folk tradition, the biblical figure Moses has symbolized the socio-religious aspect of the consummate conjure doctor. Theologian Theophus Smith identifies the characteristics of three deities from the Yoruba pantheon of orisha that correspond to black conceptions and formations of Moses: Ifa or Orunla functions as the "diviner" who, like Moses, has the ability to prophesize, while Osanyin or Osain signifies the "herbalist" which corresponds to Moses' ability to manipulate roots and engage in hoodoo doctoring. Lastly, corresponding to the messenger and or trickster is Eshu or Elegba who is analogous to Moses' position as God's chief communicant and magician.[1]

Harriet Tubman, often associated with the "liberating" character of Moses, also exhibited a talent for divination and root working while claiming to be a gifted medium for God's messages and instructions. Though Tubman was given the monikers "General Moses" and "the Moses of her people" there has not been a scholarly discussion on the fullness of her "Mosaic" character beyond her efforts to make perilous journeys back to the slave territories to rescue scores of others held in bondage.[2] As significant as her "liberating" feats were, they would not have been possible without Tubman drawing on what she believed were her divinely endowed faculties that allowed her to hear God's voice and work "miracles" in a similar fashion to Moses and his orisha counterparts. It is suggested here that Tubman's correlation to Moses can be attributed to the persistence of African religious beliefs expressed through the guise of Moses' heroic role in the biblical story of Exodus.[3]

The fact that a great many blacks made Moses a relevant hero to their own plight and applied this sacred vision to Tubman allows us to assess Tubman's "Mosaic" persona through the biblical history from which slaves drew. Zora Neale Hurston, from whom quite a bit of the biblical history comes, was a trained anthropologist and folklorist of some distinction, capable of applying a certain rigor to her research and findings, and to her interpretations. She, therefore, like her nineteenth-century forebears, took the sacred texts seriously. Hurston's work and the research of others provide a conceptual framework for Tubman's connection to Moses.

Unlike Frederick Douglass, William Wells Brown, and a small number of other nineteenth-century blacks, Harriet Tubman did not enjoy the privilege of literacy and was thus unable to leave behind any written records. As is often the case with studies on slavery, the student of Tubman must piece together her story through what others have had to say about her. While such sources present a skewed portrait of Tubman, three scholars who have recently written on her have scrupulously combed through her biographical memoirs, oral testimonies, local court records, and other relevant documents in an attempt to capture who she was beyond the mythical figure that has been ingrained in American memory. These include Jean Humez's *Harriet Tubman: The Life and the Life Stories* (2003), Kate Larson's *Bound For The Promise Land: Harriet Tubman, Portrait of An American Hero* (2004), and Catherine Clinton's *Harriet Tubman: The Road To Freedom* (2004).[4] This much needed resurgence of Tubman scholarship ties together her life in slavery, tireless work on the Underground Railroad, spiritual views, efforts to assist Union forces during the Civil War, and the grassroots endeavors she involved herself in until her death in 1917. These monographs fill a gap that has existed since journalist Earl Conrad wrote *General Harriet Tubman* in 1943.[5] Prior to these new works the only writings on Tubman that succeeded Conrad's biography were comprised of fictionalized children's literature.[6]

The first accounts of Tubman appeared in the 1860s and of these Sarah Bradford authored the most comprehensive treatment in *Scenes in the Life of Harriet Tubman* (1869) which was later revised as *Harriet, the Moses of Her People* (1886 and 1901). Franklin Sanborn and Ednah Cheney wrote the other two brief accounts in anti-slavery newspapers in 1863 and 1865, respectively.[7] While Sanborn and Cheney enjoyed a personal relationship with Tubman, Bradford was the only biographer who interviewed her. Humez persuasively argues that this allowed Tubman, who was already an experienced oral autobiographer on the anti-slavery lecture circuit, to exert some control over her own voice by choosing which stories to tell Bradford. More than simply a third person anecdotal account, Bradford's mediated autobiographical text provides us with what has come to be known as Tubman's slave narrative. Despite its shortcomings it is the best example of Tubman's own text. Humez also maintains that Tubman "authored" her autobiography through her songs, stories, and dramatic reenactments all of which are essential pieces of her larger narrative.[8]

Humez and Larson provide extensive analyses of Tubman's spirituality. While neither offers a sustained discussion of the impact that African spiritual beliefs may have had on Tubman, Larson does concede that African cultural traditions along with evangelical Protestantism were responsible for shaping Tubman's spiritual views. Larson, for example, makes the salient point that African-born slaves, like Tubman's grandmother Modesty, served as "a living African connection and memory for Tubman and her family." She also notes that the slaves' interpretation of the bible reflected a worldview molded by both African and American influences. The ideas espoused by black spirituals, for instance, often ran counter to white interpretations of the Holy Scripture. Black evangelicals were inclined to draw on the Old Testament to help fashion the belief that they were God's chosen people.[9]

This chapter seeks to broaden our understanding of Tubman's connection to African culture as it relates to African-American folk notions of Moses. Harriet Tubman's self-proclaimed gifts of prophecy and ability to work "magical" wonders along with her belief that she was a chosen conduit for the voice of God were inextricably linked to one another. Convinced that she was able to transform her own reality and the lives of others through her divinely inspired dreams, visions, and premonitions, Tubman as a seer, like the Yoruba orisha Ifa or Orunla, claimed that there was never a time when she did not feel the presence of God surrounding her. She did not engage in typical morning and evening prayer rituals. Rather, when she felt the need for divine intervention she spoke to God just "as a man talketh with his friend" and firmly trusted that her loyal companion and protector would assist her whenever she was in need of help.[10]

Ednah Cheney reported that many of Tubman visions often came to her while she was working in the field:

> She once said, 'We'd been carting manure all day, and the other girl and I were going home on the sides of the cart, and another boy was driving, when suddenly I heard such music as filled all the air;' and she saw a vision which she described in language which sounded like the old prophets in its grand flow; interrupted now and then by what the other girl said, by Master's coming and calling her, to wake up, and her protests that she wasn't asleep.[11]

Though it is not known whether or not Tubman was listening to the nearby sounds of a ring shout ceremony or the musical voices of other field laborers when she had this particular vision, the connection between the music she heard that "filled all the air" and her esoteric experience was very much in accordance with black spirituality.[12]

Sarah Bradford declared that she witnessed "such *remarkable* instances of what seemed to be her direct intercourse with heaven."[13] One gets the sense that Bradford observed scenes in which Tubman was doing more than simply praying out loud. Perhaps these "remarkable" experiences involved a change in Tubman's physical appearance as her spirit seemed to be mounted by the Supreme Deity; what W.E.B. DuBois refers to as the frenzy.[14] Whatever the case, they certainly were not mundane episodes.

In a letter written to Bradford, abolitionist Thomas Garret expressed similar sentiments to those of his anti-slavery colleague: "I never met with any person, of any color, who had more confidence in the voice of God, as spoken direct to her soul. She has frequently told me that she talked with

God, and he talked with her every day of her life."[15] That Tubman left such a profound impression on Garret for which he could find no comparison suggests that the he too witnessed Tubman's scenes which were nothing short of extraordinary.

Tubman often interpreted the "voice" of God that she claimed to hear as forewarnings that she should act with caution and prudence. Her spirit became disturbed on one particular occasion when she intuitively *felt* that three of her brothers were facing the prospect of being sold to the deep South. Much like the orisha Eshu or Elegba known for their role as trickster and God's messenger, Tubman cunningly managed to get word to her brothers that they were to begin making preparations for their escape. She asked a friend to write a coded letter to Jacob Jackson who was a literate free black residing near her brothers' plantation. Self-elected inspectors of correspondence screened Jacob's mail because he was under suspicion for helping others escape and for this reason Tubman knew she had to be especially careful with this mission.[16]

The secret meaning of the letter was contained in the closing: "Read my letter to the old folks, and give my love to them, and tell my brothers to be always *watching unto prayer,* and when *the good old ship of Zion comes along, to be ready to step on board.*" Tubman employed her friend to sign the letter "William Henry Jackson" who was the son of Jacob Jackson. The letter made little sense to the inspectors who knew that William did not have parents or brothers. When Jacob was summoned to read the letter, he quickly grasped the inferential meaning that "Moses" was on her way. Shrewdly, he acted as if he too was confused by the contents of the note. "Dat letter can't be meant for me no how," he said as he threw it down "I can't make head or tail of it."[17]

Realizing that he had little time, Jacob rushed to inform Tubman's brothers to prepare for their sister's arrival and be on the look out for her signal to head North. When Tubman appeared unannounced on Christmas Eve she did in fact learn as she had prophetically suspected that her brothers were to be carted off to the South the next day. She swiftly and successfully stole them away under the cover of darkness.[18] Tubman's ability to confront this dangerous risk in the face of seemingly insurmountable odds would have been enough for others to think of her as their Moses leading them to the promise land. But those who followed her would have also been able to appreciate her knack for deception. As a trickster and or magician relying on the voice of God to effect change much like the Yoruba orisha Eshu or Elegba, Tubman's actions bear resemblances to Moses' conjuring tricks.[19] It was said that Tubman "magically" appeared on the plantation and then suddenly vanished without being noticed by anyone except for those involved in the rescue.[20]

On another one of Tubman's rescue missions while leading a band of men to the North she again became shrouded with an ominous feeling that something was wrong. She felt it necessary that the group change course and cross a river that was flowing rather rapidly. With no bridge or boat to assist them, those in her camp voiced their concerns about the depth of the unfriendly waters. Fearless and determined, Tubman began to tread her way to the other side and the others followed. "De water never came above my chin" she says "when we thought surely we were all going under, it became shallower and shallower, and we came out safe on the odder side."[21] After successfully traversing another stream the group came upon a posted notice of their escape and learned that had they not heeded Tubman's suggestion to pursue a new path they would have indeed been captured by the slave patrol.

Thomas Garret corroborated Tubman's story. "When she called on me two days after" he disclosed "she was so hoarse she could hardly speak, and was also suffering with a violent toothache." Garret also indicated that the owners of the men who Tubman was leading to the North were responsible for posting the advertisement which offered a reward for their detainment.[22] This expedition is another example of the liberating character of Tubman's Mosaic identity. It also in some ways represents Moses' magical nature as God's messenger corresponding to the orisha Eshu or Elegba. Tubman listened to the "voice" of God to lead her people out of slavery across an ostensibly impassable body of water in the same way God in the story of Exodus instructed Moses to stretch out his rod and part the red sea to safely guide the Israelites out of Egypt. Like Pharaoh's horsemen, the slave hunters who pursued Tubman were thrown off course.

At other times Tubman claimed to have uncannily known that certain people, including Garret, had the exact amount of money or close to it that she could use to help those who were in need of her assistance. "God tells me you have money for me," she once revealed to him. When Garret inquired of the amount Tubman desired she took a moment to study the matter as if she was receiving a divine message and indicated that approximately twenty-three dollars would suffice. Garret then gave her a little more than twenty-four dollars from which he collected from Eliza Wigham who was the Secretary of a Scotland-based Anti-Slavery society. When Garret told others about Tubman's efforts to help slaves, one man offered to send her the money by way of Ms. Wigham. Tubman believed that these acts of altruism were a testimony to her visionary prowess and *special* relationship with God.[23]

A year later Tubman told Garret she was divinely informed that he once again had some funds available for her. *Somehow* she knew that the amount this time was not as great as before. Garret had in fact received a smaller amount from Europe for Tubman just a few days prior to her visit. Tubman's amazing ability to *know things* left quite an impression on Garret. He wrote "to say the least there was something remarkable in these facts, whether clairvoyance, or the divine impression on her mind from the source of all power, I cannot tell; but certain it was she had a guide within herself other than the written word, for she never had an education." Tubman, like Moses, believed that these intimations that came to her were vital to her efforts in freeing her fellow bondsmen and women.[24]

She was able to free her father in a similar fashion. When she received a vision "in some mysterious or supernatural way" that some of the elderly folk were in danger she visited the office of a New York abolitionist of which she was acquainted and told him that God had sent her there to receive the money she needed for her next mission. The agent declared that God must have had it wrong this time as he had no money for her. Convinced that God had not led her astray she was resolved to remain in the gentleman's office without food or drink until she was given twenty dollars in order that she could go retrieve "de old people."[25] When she awakened from a deep slumber to which she was often subjected since the days of her childhood head injury she learned that a number of visitors to the office had kindly left her sixty dollars. With this generous gift she headed south again only to learn that her father was to be tried in court the following week for providing aid to runaways. She related in a forceful tone, "I just removed my father's trial to a higher court, and brought him off to Canada."[26]

Tubman would later have another vision involving the tragic death of the daughter of abolitionist William H. Seward, Frances Seward.[27] Frances lived in Auburn New York, but was visiting her father in Washington at the time. Tubman claimed to have witnessed "a chariot in the air, going south, and empty, but soon it returned, and lying in it, cold and stiff, was the body." Tubman hastily made her way to Auburn to inform folk that "Oh, Miss Fanny is dead!" Again, her suspicions were confirmed when she learned that the people there had just learned of Frances's passing.[28]

Harriet Tubman's contemporary William Wells Brown discussed in our previous chapter also witnessed her extraordinary intimations. He writes:

> While in Canada, in 1860, we met several whom this woman had brought from the land of bondage, and they all believed that she had supernatural power. Of one man we inquired, "Were you not afraid of being caught?" "Oh, no," he said, "Moses is got de charm." "What do you mean?" we asked. He replied, "De whites can't catch Moses, kase you see she's born wid de charm. De Lord has given Moses de power."

"Yes," Brown added "and the woman herself felt that she had the charm, and this feeling, no doubt, nerved her up, gave her courage, and made all who followed her feel safe in her hands." Brown's passage reveals the way in which the slave community viewed Tubman's "Mosaic" persona. For those who depended on Tubman and were intimately familiar with her, she was more than the embodiment of Moses; she was Moses.[29]

Our understanding of the biblical Moses in the black folk tradition is further illuminated by the ethnographic accounts and literary writings of folklorists Zora Neale Hurston along with other contemporaneous discussions on the significance of Moses in African-American folk culture. These sources provide a cultural framework for examining the fullness of Tub-man's "Mosaic" character.[30]

In *Mules and Men* (1935) Hurston explains how the biblical creation story of *Genesis* was appropriated as a conjure story in the black folk tradition. She writes:

> Belief in magic is older than writing. So nobody knows how it started. The way we tell it, hoodoo started way back there before everything. Six days of magic spells and mighty words and the world with its elements above and below was made. And now, God is leaning back taking a seventh day rest. When the eighth day comes around, He'll start to making new again.[31]

Hurston stresses the African-American folk notion that only Moses was granted the wisdom to know the secrets of God's wondrous works. He "was the first man who ever learned God's power-compelling words and it took him forty years to learn ten words."[32]

Harry Middleton Hyatt's study on African-American folklore resonates with Zora Neale Hurston's analysis of Moses as a transatlantic deity associated with hoodoo in the United States. In his two-volume series *Hoodoo-Conjuration-Witchcraft-Rootwork* Hyatt includes the account of a New Orleans informant referred to as "Hoodoo Book Man" because he was versed in the *The Sixth and Seventh Books of Moses*. Hoodo Book Man offered an interpretation similar to Hurston's concerning the ancient origins of Hoodoo:

> Hoodooism started way back in de time dat Moses days, back in ole ancient times, nine thousand years ago. Now you see, Moses, he was a prophet jis' like Peter, Paul an' James. An' den he quit bein' a prophet an' started de hoodooism—what we call de *Seven Book of Moses*. See, I read de Seven Book of Moses seven or eight year a'ready. You take de *Seven Book of Moses*—well aftah Moses writ de *Seven Book of Moses*, dere where hoodooism took about.[33]

He then offered some hoodoo prescriptions with "John De Conker root" and concluded by returning to the point that "de foundation of hoodoosim came from back yondah de time dat Moses written de book—*De Seven Book of Moses*."

Harriet Tubman's expressed similar sentiments in her most explicit self-proclaimed connection to Moses:

> Long ago when the Lord told me to go free my people, I said, "No, Lord! I can't go—don't ask me." But he come another time. I saw him just as plain. Then I said again, "Lord, go away—get some better educated person—get a person with more culture than I have; go away,

Lord." But he came back the third time, and speaks to me just as he did to Moses, and he says, "Harriet, I want you." I knew then I must do what he bid me. Now do you suppose he wanted me to do this just for a day, or a week? No! the Lord who told me take care of my people meant me to do it just so long as I live, and so I do what he told me to."[34]

Here Tubman establishes a connection between her initial reluctance and insecure feelings about serving as the agent and voice of God and Moses' similar experience when he first heard God speak through the burning bush. Moses, like Tubman, also had reservations. While Tubman felt that she was sufficiently lacking education and culture, Moses worried that he was not eloquent enough to speak on behalf of God and feared that the Egyptians would have little faith in his word.[35]

God ultimately persuaded Moses to accept his divine instruction that he was the chosen one to free the Israelites and Tubman became convinced that she was the right person to help the southern slaves. As extraordinary as this endeavor was for Tubman, the perceived magical ability to hear God's words in the same way the Yoruba orisha Eshu or Elegba functioned as God's chief communicant contributed Tubman's Mosaic identity.

Part of this identity can also be attributed to Harriet Tubman's relationship to her father Benjamin Ross. She claimed that it was he who bequeathed to her his special gift of being able to sense what was going to occur in the future. According to Tubman, not only was he always able to predict the weather, Benjamin also prophesized the Mexican War before it occurred.[36] Hurston explores a similar relationship that existed between Moses and his father in-law Jethro of Midan in her historical novel *Moses: Man of the Mountain* (1939).

In the introduction she suggests that there are clear differences between the conception of Moses in the traditional Christian and Judaic world and how he is perceived throughout the African Diaspora. She explains that in the African worldview Moses was more than "the great law-giver" who challenged Pharaoh and led the Israelites out of Egypt. He was the quintessential mystic man who conversed with the Supreme Deity and used "his rod of power" as an instrument of magical sorcery. Like Hyatt's interviewee "Hoodoo Book Man," Hurston claims that many of those who considered Moses in this light were secretly consulting *The Sixth and Seventh Books of Moses*, of which there were millions of copies.[37] She asserts that African religions and social thought informed the ways in which Moses related to the needs of blacks in the Diaspora. It is for this reason that Jethro, a high-priest of Midian, like Tubman's father, was also viewed as "a great hoodoo man." Moses as an apprentice under him learned the mysteries of divine magic.

In Hurston's historical novel Jethro intuitively knew Moses' name before it was told to him. On another occasion when the two were first getting to know each other Jethro informed Moses that his oldest daughter was named Zipporah. It surprised Moses that Jethro mentioned this at the precise moment when he was thinking about her and said "that is the second time that you have read my mind, Jethro. You must teach me how to do that." Jethro explained to Moses that the secret mysteries of mind reading and divination were not things that men could simply learn, but were rather gifts from God. Jethro told him that he *knew* Moses was born with the gift of the greatest magic that could transform the plight of the downtrodden.[38]

Hurston presents a Moses who was drawn to Midian because of the sense of security and familiarity it offered him. This was the place of refugee that he had frequently visualized since childhood. "He had been here often," Hurston writes "by some mysterious forecast of dreams." The people he encountered were not strange or foreign to him. He even spoke the dialect of the people with ease.[39] Tubman had a similar dream about the North that could have lent further credence to the notion that she, albeit a female, symbolized and was the contemporary Moses.

Prior to her escape she often dreamt of flying "like a bird" over a diverse landscape which came to signify her flight to the North. In her dream she would approach a barrier either in the form of a huge fence or a river above which she would attempt to soar. "But it' peared like I wouldn't hab de strength" she says "and jes as I was sinkin' down, dere would be ladies all drest in white ober dere, and de would put out dere arms and pull me 'cross."[40] When she eventually reached the North, like Moses when he reached Midian, she came face to face with the places and people she observed in her dreams.[41]

Tubman's reference to flight might have been more than just an allegory for her escape. The motif of the flying African may actually be at work here. As discussed in chapter one it was not uncommon for slaves to draw on the Igbo notion of the soul actually returning to Africa through flight. The Bight of Biafra contributed significant imports into North America and Igbo from the region were largely responsible for spreading the belief.[42] Tubman's recurring dream may offer a new perspective on the tales of flying Africans. Though she did not return to Africa in her vision, she did make it to the North which in her mind was as good a safe heaven as any. Sarah Bradford also claimed that Tubman often imagined "that her 'spirit' leaves her body, and visits other scenes and places, not only in this world but in the world of the spirits."[43]

When Thomas Smith of Yamacraw, Georgia, was interviewed during the 1930s, he drew an intriguing link between the belief in the magical authority of Moses and the idea that blacks could fly. He believed that the power Moses used to transform rods into snakes in Pharaoh's court still existed among blacks and went on to claim:

Dat happen in Africa duh Bible say. Ain dat show dat Africa wuz a lan uh magic powuh since duh beginning uh history. Well den, duh descendants ub Africans hab duh same gif tuh do unnatchul ting. Ise heahd duh story uh duh flyin Africans an I sho belieb it happen."[44]

Smith did not differentiate between Moses' power and the ability of blacks to fly, boil water without fire, and command a buzzard to row a boat. His testimony corroborates the contention that this sense of interconnectedness permeated the black folk tradition and suggests that Harriet Tubman's dream of flying North was very much related to her Mosaic persona.

This persona was reinforced by Tubman's association with her legendary gun. The musket that Tubman is holding in the picture reproduced for Bradford's book has come to represent her militancy in American cultural memory and is also a sort of allegory for Moses' magical rod. Hurston says "ever since the days of Moses kings have been toting rods for a sign of power. But it's mostly sham-polish because no king has ever had the power of even one of Moses' ten words."[45] Tubman's gun, which was probably a revolver on this occasion rather than the larger musket with which she is usually associated, could have easily reminded those men and women she led to the North of Moses' rod.[46] While Moses' rod gave him the power to fashion snakes, ruin the drinking water of the Egyptians, create plagues and pestilences, and part the red sea, Tubman used her pistol for purposes of security and deterrence. Members of Tubman's party were threatened if deemed a potential detriment to forward progress in symbolically the same way Moses demonstrated to the Egyptians that they would have a heavy price to pay if they kept the Israelites in slavery.

When Ednah Cheney asked Tubman if she really intended to shoot anyone she replied "yes if he was weak enough to give out, he'd be weak enough to betray us all, and all who had helped us; and do you think I'd let so many die just for one coward man?" She recalled the time when one fugitive declared his swollen and pain-ridden feet would prevent him from continuing with the group. Even after receiving medical attention and words of encouragement he was still determined to return to his master's quarters. Tubman had the remedy. She "told the boys to get their guns ready, and shoot him." Her lieutenants were ready to act, but when he heard her orders he "jumped right up and went on as well as anybody."[47] Tubman informed Bradford in her 1869 edition that "dead niggers tell no tales, go on or die" as she herself aimed the revolver at those who refused to stay with the band.[48] As commander and chief of these expeditions Tubman's gun, like Moses' connection to his rod, was an extension of her personality.

Hurston continued to examine Moses in her anthropological study *Tell My Horse* (1838) which examined the practice of Voodoo in Haiti and Jamaica. In this work she addressed the incorporation of Moses in a particular Haitian pantheon of deities (*loas* or *mysteres*). Hurston explained that Damballah (or Damballah Ouedo Freda Tocan Dahomey), the primary deity in Haiti, is acknowledged as Moses, whose avatar is the serpent.

There is also evidence that Damballah was also worshiped in Louisiana.[49] Hurston writes:

> This worship of Moses recalls the hard-to-explain fact that wherever the Negro is found, there are traditional tales of Moses and his supernatural powers that are not in the Bible, nor can they be found in any written life of Moses. The rod of Moses is said to have been a subtle serpent and hence came his great powers. All over the Southern United States, the British West Indies and Haiti there are reverent tales of Moses and his magic.[50]

Hurston theorized that there were probably age-old tales throughout Africa and Asia that Moses was the "great father of magic." It was from African examples, however, that Hurston drew parallels. She noted that there were witch doctors all over the continent that, like Moses and his rod, were believed to have had the ability to entrance serpents and transform them into lifeless canes. Disputing claims that followers of Damballah worshiped the snake, Hurston explained that it is rather revered as the servant of the deity and for this reason is protected and honored.[51] Throughout her travels she was struck by the ubiquitous presence of altars honoring Damballah that were adorned with actual snakes or iron replicas of them.

We learn from a prophetic recurring dream that Harriet Tubman had involving the militant anti-slavery advocate John Brown that there is evidence that she may have also been associated with "snake wisdom." Tubman's extraordinary success in bringing men and women out of bondage without getting caught captured the attention of Brown.[52] The two were introduced in the fugitive slave community of St. Catherines Canada.

Brown was impressed with what he heard of Tubman's exploits and believed that she would serve as a good adviser for his scheme of erecting a new state for freed slaves in the mountainous regions of Virginia and western Maryland because of her extensive knowledge of the Maryland and Pennsylvania routes of the Underground Railroad. He might have also felt that given Tubman's familiarity with slaves and newly freed persons on both sides of the border that she could successfully recruit others to join the plot. General Tubman, as Brown called her, was drawn to his message of freedom at any cost. That he, like her, claimed to have received his convictions directly from God may have provided Tubman with a sense that his mission also was a divine one.[53]

Just prior to meeting Brown for the first time Tubman had a dream that she would later come to interpret as a warning from God.

> She thought she was in 'a wilderness sort of place, all full of rocks, and bushes,' when she saw a serpent raise its head of an old man with a long white beard, gazing at her, 'wishful like, jes as ef he war gwine to speak to me,' and then two other heads rose up beside him, younger

than he—and as she stood looking at them, and wondering what they could want with her, a great crowd of men rushed in and struck down the younger heads, and then the head of the old man, still looking at her so 'wishful.'[54]

Tubman did not fully understand the meaning of the dream until after Brown's attack on Harpers Ferry. It is fairly well known that his men proved no match for an outfit of U.S. Marines led by Robert E. Lee. Ten of Brown's soldiers were killed including his two sons Watson and Oliver. Some of the others were captured and only a few, including Brown, managed to escape. All were eventually arrested and awaited trial for treason and igniting a slave rebellion.[55]

Though Tubman was in New York when the incident occurred she had one of her *feelings* that something was not right. After brooding over the matter for some time she informed her hostess that "Captain Brown" must be in trouble and that she expected to hear something dreadful regarding his fate. On the following day she heard the tragic details of the attack from those who learned of them from a local newspaper.[56] It was then that she finally understood the meaning of her dream that she had had so many times. The two younger heads of the serpent that were struck down by the great crowd represented the fall of Brown's sons at the hands of Lee and his men. The elder head symbolized Brown who would be ultimately tried and hanged.[57]

Tubman was not known to keep her dreams or visions to herself.[58] Ednah Cheney observed that Tubman "loves to describe her visions, which are very real to her; but she must tell them word for word as they lie in her untutored mind, with endless repetitions and details."[59] While Tubman's dream was quite different from Moses' exploits in Pharaoh's palace, her account calls to mind the story of Exodus. Moses' transformation of rods into snakes was a significant phase in a series of magical acts which ultimately led to the end of Egyptian slavery. Tubman indicated that the serpents were a symbol of the freedom for which Brown and his sons fought and her imagery of the wilderness and the bush call to mind Moses' interaction with God through the burning bush.

Other sources corroborate Hurston's claim that snakes were part of the iconographic and spiritual culture of blacks.[60] Carver James Cooper of Yamacraw, Georgia, also known as "Stick Daddy," told interviewers during the 1930s that he believed he inherited his grandfather's skill who was adept at crafting baskets, chairs, tables and other things from wood and straw. "Stick Daddy" had a particular knack for making wooden canes, one of which was a "snake-encircled rod with a handle made from a large black and white die." He also knew how to fix things and claimed to have a few "sho cuos" for illnesses.[61]

Writing on the inhabitants of Southern Nigeria Major, Arthur Glen Leonard found that the dreaming of a snake meant that the one's enemies were seeking to cause tremendous harm and quite possibly death to the dreamer. It was believed that this was caused by an "evil" or "antipathetic" spirit who visited the person having the dream.[62] Susie Branch of White Bluff Georgia explained that such dreams held a similar meaning. She divulged that Sukey, one of her esteemed ancestors, was the head seamstress for the slaves on St. Catherines Island who was stolen "frum off duh beach in Africa wen she wuz a young miss." When queried on whether or not the dreaming of snakes bore any significance she responded, "yes, ma'am, dat mean yuh got a enemy. Not many nights ago I dram bout a snake an uh sho wuz sked wen uh wake up."[63]

Mini Dawson of Pin Point Island Georgia provided a similar account. "Ef yuh dream ub a snake dassa enemy neahby too."[64] Though Harriet Tubman was not specifically targeted at Harpers Ferry, those responsible for bringing down John Brown and his cohorts in many ways represented the opposing forces to everything for which she stood. Thus, her dream of snakes and their association with one's adversary was very much in accord with others who were also influenced by African culture. Snakes were associated with conjuration and hoodoo. Nathaniel John Lewis of Tin City, Georgia, for example, revealed that his wife Hattie "had a spell put on uh fuh three long yeahs with a nest of rattlesnakes inside uh." She was unable to eat and would foam at the mouth like a snake releasing venom.[65]

Tubman believed that she did in fact have a "hand" in the death of her master, Edward Brodess. When rumors around the slave quarters surfaced that Brodess was seeking to sell Tubman to the deep south to work on a chain gang she asked God that he convert her master to a kind-loving Christian gentleman bestowing upon him a change of heart regarding her sale. When her fears of being sold became a reality she asked God to take Brodess's life if he was not to be proselytized. "Next ting I heard ole master was dead" she says "and he died just as he had lived, a wicked, bad man." [66]

The implication that Tubman had a hand in her master's demise mirrors the prototypical conjure figure who wished to rid their community of malevolent forces. As a gifted healer, visionary, and self-professed communicant with God, Tubman represented the epitome of such an individual. Here it is instructive to recall the analogy that Theophus Smith draws between the Yoruba orisha Osanyin or Osain in their role as the herbalist and the African-American folk notion of Moses in his similar role as an herbal doctor or 'root worker' capable of healing and harming through hoodoo.[67] In this instance Tubman's prayers were the tools needed for her "hoodoo."

Tubman also demonstrated her skills in the curative art of "roots" while working as a nurse for the Union forces during the Civil War. She was known to have come to the aid of many soldiers who suffered from life-threatening ailments in the Port Royal area of South Carolina.[68] Her remedy often entailed seeking out roots and herbs that were harvested in close proximity to where the disease originated. In this role as a conjure doctor, she had a cunning knack for curing dysentery, small-pox, and malignant fevers—never once acquiring any of the illnesses she treated.[69]

Tubman also labored as an unpaid recruiter, scout, and spy for the Union during the war at the request of General Andrews of Massachusetts. As a spy she was not afraid to penetrate into the deep southern war zones and obtain valuable information about the positions of armies and batteries and relay her findings to Generals Stevens, Sherman, and Hunter. Her military prowess is remarkably close to Hurston's description of Moses as a born military general who successfully experimented with troop placement and maneuvers.[70]

Tubman was the first woman to spearhead an attack on a confederate stronghold. Acting as the chief advisor to Colonel James Montgomery, commander of the Second South Carolina regiment, Tubman led the African-American infantry twenty-five miles up South Carolina's Combahee River to rebel warehouses of rice and cotton.[71] Colonel Montgomery's men disabled Confederate gunners, torched plantations, homes, railroad bridges, and factories and seized about a thousand dollars in stores. Realizing that this may have been their only chance of escaping their masters' whips and pistols which were being brandished at this time in an attempt to prevent them from leaving, at least eight hundred determined slaves hastily made their way for Colonel Montgomery's gun-boats and were transported to Beaufort. Tubman said that she had never seen nothing like it:

> Here you'd see a woman wid a pail on her head, rice a smokin' in it jus' as she'd taken it from de fire, young one hangin' on behind, one han' roun' her forehead to hold on, 'tother han' diggin' into de rice-pot, eatin' wid all its might; hold of her dress two or three more . . . Sometimes de women would come wid twins hangin' roun' der necks; 'pears like I nebber see so many twins in my life; bags on der shoulders, baskets on der heads, an young ones taggin' behin', all loaded.[72]

While on board the boat Tubman, at the request of Colonel Montgomery, sang a song to ease the nerves of the fugitives:

> *Of all the whole creation in the East or in the West,*
> *The glorious Yankee nation is the greatest and the best.*
> *Come along! Come along! Don't be alarmed,*
> *Uncle Sam is rich enough to give you all a farm.*[73]

Maintaining a pattern of call and response that was typical of slave singing, the escapees raised their hands and cried "Glory" after each verse.

Tubman actually became quite fond of the religious and cultural practices of the South Carolina sea island blacks during the war. She spoke passionately about the "very peculiar dialect" of black preachers, the songs she heard at camp-meetings, her impressions of "experience meetings," and the dances she observed at midnight funeral ceremonies. Tubman remembered that after one preacher delivered his sermon at a funeral ceremony the entire congregation while shaking hands and calling each by name engaged in a circular solemn dance known as the "spiritual shuffle" at which time they sang:

> *My sis'r Mary's boun' to go;*
> *My sis'r Nanny's boun' to go;*
> *My brudder Tony's boun't to go;*
> *My brudder July's boun' to go.*[74]

Harriet, a stranger among the faithful, was a participant in this ring shout ceremony and when it came time for her name to be called during the song they sang *"Eberybody's boun' to go!"*[75] Circle dances at burial sites were frequent occurrences throughout the south.[76] Tubman's recollection of "shaking hands" and calling out names resembles the 1930s description of Alec Anderson, a ring shout participant from Possum Point Georgia. "We dance round shake the hand and fiddle the feet," he disclosed "one of us kneel down in the middle of the circle. Then we all call out and rise and shout around, and we all fling the foot again."[77] Because the ring shout lied at the core of black spiritual practices, most among of the slave class would have agreed that Tubman's involvement in the ceremony was in sync with the qualities and character of Moses. Possession or spiritual mounting, the high point of the ring shout, was not remarkably different from the idea that Moses entranced serpents. Tubman, much like her biblical counterpart in the black folk tradition, embraced the supernatural.

Tubman had another premonition three years before the first shot was fired on Fort Sumter. It happened while she was staying at the home of black abolitionist Rev. Henry Highland Garnet in New York. As mentioned in our treatment of Frederick Douglass and William Wells Brown, Garnet's 1843 radical *Address to the Slaves of the United States of America* called for a slave uprising and a general strike to improve the conditions of blacks throughout the country. Considering some of the similarities between John Brown's views and those of Garnet it makes sense that Tubman and the latter were able to forge a close bond. The vision she received at her comrade's home involved the emancipation of the slaves:

> She rose singing, 'My people are free!' 'My, people are free!' She came down to breakfast singing the words in a sort of ecstasy. She could not eat. The dream or vision filled her whole soul, and physical needs were forgotten.[78]

When General Rufus Saxton, the Union military governor of the Department of the South, decided to host a festival on New Years Day in the Port Royal district celebrating Lincoln's signing of the 1863 Emancipation

Proclamation a number of blacks from the various Sea Islands took to the streets to participate in this grand gala. While most were enjoying the merriment, Tubman was asked why she was not taking part in the festivities. She explained "I had my jubilee three years ago. I rejoiced all I could den; I can't rejoice no more."[79] Tubman also understood that the war was far from over and that she must continue fighting because most of her people were still in shackles.[80] After the war, Tubman devoted her time to suffrage, and religious and humanitarian movements. In 1896 she founded a home and hospital for blacks who were improvised, ill, and elderly and later worked with the African Methodist Episcopal church.[81]

Through her insightful descriptions of slave dance and song, her revealing accounts of her visions and dreams, her healing prowess during the Civil War, and her self-proclaimed intimate conversations with God, Tubman was more deeply African and "Mosaic" than previously thought. While not much is known of her affiliation with the church during her years in slavery, she was occasionally required to attend the services of her master's son Anthony Thompson. Tubman's parents maintained a strong faith in God and they were convinced that Anthony's clerical exploits were insincere. Tubman's own religious beliefs were largely shaped by her parents. Tubman considered herself to be a true follower of Christ. However, like many antebellum blacks she thought of her religion as quite different from that which was generally practiced by the planter class.[82]

Like Frederick Douglass, William Wells Brown, Harriet Jacobs, and most nineteenth-century blacks who authored slave narratives, this commitment to Christianity did not preclude her from embracing those beliefs and customs that her forebears carried across the Atlantic. This may be most evident by her assertion that her special abilities were inherited from her father. Her relationship is analogous to the close bond that Douglass shared with his grandmother who was also immersed in African culture. Moreover, Tubman claimed to have received periodic hints of the future as did one of Douglass's closest confidants, Sandy Jenkins. For Tubman, more than was the case for anyone else, her African sensibility aided her in helping scores of others. Beginning in 1850, the year the Fugitive Slave Act was enacted, to about 1860 Tubman returned to Maryland roughly thirteen times to liberate approximately seventy family members and friends. While this is the most obvious connection that Tubman had to her "Mosaic" persona it certainly was not, as we have seen, the only one.

4 Harriet Jacobs
A Larger Discussion of the John Kuner Parade and Other Cultural Recollections

Harriet Jacobs's memoir *Incidents in the Life of a Slave Girl* (1861), pub-lished under the pseudonym Linda Brent, was the first full length slave nar-rative authored by a woman and is one of the most harrowing testimonies from the nineteenth century. The text received its fair share of commentary during the time it was written and was considered a legitimate source by contemporary reviewers. However, it remained in relative obscurity during most of the twentieth century until the Harcourt Brace Jovanovich edi-tion appeared in 1973.[1] The reemergence of Jacobs's narrative sparked an immediate debate over its authenticity. Jean Yellin settled the dispute when she made the groundbreaking discovery in 1981 of letters that Jacobs had written to abolitionist and women's rights activist Amy Post. This gave historians and literary critics sufficient evidence to designate the text as a reputable resource in the annals of American slavery.[2]

When Yellin edited *Incidents* in 1987 she not only began to solidify her-self as the premier scholar on Jacobs, she also sparked a renewed interest in her. Jacobs's acceptance of Christianity, the degree to which she was able to assert her own voice throughout her text, the ways in which she confronted and overcame gender norms and sexual exploitation, and the relationship her narrative had to other slave narratives as well as other literary genres are among the key issues to which scholars have devoted their attention.[3]

Yellin published her second edition of *Incidents* in 2000 and recently wrote the first biography of Jacobs, *Harriet Jacobs: A Life* (2004). In the latter work Yellin chronicles Harriet Jacobs's later involvement in the anti-slavery and women's rights movement as well as her relief work with her daughter during the post-slavery years in which she erected schools and hospitals for black refugees in D.C., Virginia, and Savannah. Yellin also provides insightful revelations of Jacobs's brother John who in addition to authoring his own slave narrative served as a primary inspiration for Jacobs's participation in the anti-slavery movement as he himself worked closely with Frederick Douglass and other high ranking abolitionists.[4]

Incidents has now become the most popular women's slave narrative and scholars continue to make use of the text in intriguing ways. Drawing on the manner in which Sterling Stuckey in his essay "Ironic Tenacity: Frederick

Douglass's Seizure of the Dialectic" employed Douglass's narratives to investigate the author's observations of slave culture in nineteenth Maryland, Karen E. Beardslee in her article "Through Slave Culture's Lens Comes the Abundant Source: Harriet A. Jacobs's Incidents in the Life of a Slave Girl" strives to craft a similar cultural analysis by relying on Jacobs's text.[5]

Exploring the African social value of ancestral reverence and the sacred relationship between children and elders that were instilled in Jacobs by her grandmother Molly Horniblow and treating Jacobs's observations of the slave John Kunering festival, Beardslee breaks the mold by reaching beyond the scope of most traditional studies on Jacobs which have been primarily concerned with how her narrative advances the understanding of slave women who were faced with the dual obstacles of racial and gender oppression.[6] This chapter builds upon Beardslee's brief cultural illustration of Jacobs's narrative by showing how the text yields greater evidence that Jacobs was profoundly familiar with African culture. Jacobs, like the other individuals discussed throughout this project, was indeed drawn to an anti-slavery Christianity. Yet, like Harriet Tubman, she also had faith in visions, and her experiences with African-influenced healing folk remedies and religious dancing ceremonies, her discussion of slave conjuration and divination, her allusion to the motif of the flying African all corroborate the notion that Jacobs and the North Carolinian slave community that she wrote about had not forsaken the culture and values of their forbearers.

It also seems that Jacobs's narrative when considered alongside those of Charles Ball and Jacob Stroyer may reveal even more about the John Kunering festival. Various forms of Kunering have been documented in Jamaica, Cuba and the Bahamas. Though the consensus among scholars is that the revelry surrounding the parade which Jacobs so impressively described did not extend beyond North Carolina in the United States, it is not beyond reason to conclude that some semblance of the festival was not unfamiliar to South Carolinian slaves. Moreover, as we will explore, there is convincing evidence that the festival had an underlying meaning of escape.

In addition to the cultural matters that will be addressed, attention will also be given to the ways in which Jacobs challenged the model of plantation paternalism. Jean Yellin and others have viewed Jacobs's narrative as a radical ideological treatise written for women that portrays the author as a new kind of protagonist who successfully prevails over the culture of sexual exploitation meted out from the white patriarchy. Yellin persuasively argues that Jacobs, in her ability to manipulate her master Dr. Norcom, makes a plea for all women to shift from the "cult of domesticity" to political feminism. It is suggested here that Jacobs's radical sentiments extended even beyond gender concerns. She, like other authors of slave narratives during the Garrisonian era, made a conscious effort to critique the paternalistic views of slavery's apologists who maintained that the system was not as harsh as the abolitionists were making it out to be. Her accounts of her father and grandmother indicate that she was reared in a family that stressed a high priority on respecting familial elders over the master class.

Incidents ultimately emerges as a critical window into the cultural and political life of one of the most intriguing persons of the slavery period. The activism that Harriet Jacobs became involved in after her narrative was published was at least in part informed by the cultural and political attitudes that were ingrained in her during her formative years in the urban port city of Edenton, North Carolina. It was here that Jacobs acquired a sincere appreciation for the religious instruction she received from the three women who had the most profound impact on her spiritual views—her mother Delilah Horniblow, her maternal grandmother Molly Horniblow, who she refers to as Aunt Martha in the narrative, and her mother's owner who later became Jacobs's first mistress, Margaret Horniblow.

Harriet Jacobs was only six years old when her mother passed away and in the brief amount of time she had spent with her, one of Jacob's most treasured childhood memories was of Delilah's firm devotion to spiritual matters. Jacobs fondly recalled in her adult life the ritual of baptism through which she had been led by her mother. Jacobs also admired Delilah's decision never to desecrate the sacred vows of marriage, despite the fact that the institution was legally denied to slaves.[7] Jacobs first began to come to the understanding that she was of the slave class when her mother's death forced her to relocate to the residence of Margaret Horniblow. Compared to those slaves who labored in the field, Jacobs's lot, as was her mother's, was relatively good at Margaret's home. The mistress taught the young slave to read and sew and even impressed upon her the scriptural lessons of "love thy neighbor" and to treat others with fairness and kindness. Though Jacobs would become critical of Margaret's hypocrisy of being a slave owner later in life, at the time she believed her first mistress provided her with all of her youthful needs and wants.[8]

When Margaret passed on in 1825, Jacobs in her twelfth year had to draw her spiritual and material comfort from her grandmother as she embarked on what would become her most trying years.[9] Margaret's will stipulated that Jacobs be bequeathed to her three year old niece. This arrangement made Margaret's sister Mary and her husband Dr. Norcom Harriet's sole guardians. While Dr. Norcom was a highly respected physician and landowner in Edenton, his desire to control Jacobs with his unmerciful sexual advances, his refusal to allow her to see the man of her choice and to inadequately feed her led to Jacob's ultimate decision to escape from the Norcoms and remain hidden for nearly seven years in a diminutive, unhealthy, and poorly ventilated dwelling that was in earshot of where her children slept at night.[10]

From the time Jacobs moved in with the Norcoms until well into her adult life, her grandmother, a self-proclaimed Christian woman, remained her primary source of spiritual strength. She was active in the church and believed that Jacobs and her children should be raised with Christian values. The altruistic way in which her grandmother lived helped to embed in her mind that there was indeed a loving and just way to subscribe to Christianity. There is little doubt that the influence of her grandmother was largely responsible for the great pride that Jacobs took in bestowing Christian names upon her children.[11]

While Jacobs embraced the kind, loving, and gentle Christianity she found in her grandmother, mother, and to some degree in her first mistress, she knew that most slaves were not privy to Christian instruction and those who were, usually received a message of racial disparity from a master class who seemed to live un-Christian lives. It was the general practice of the church to keep its doors closed to the slave, and Jacobs admitted that the small number of missionaries who made their way into southern territories were looked upon with scorn and disdain. As in the other narratives treated in this study, Harriet Jacob's text provides additional evidence that the relatively little effort to Christianize blacks allowed greater room for the flourishing of African culture.[12]

Harriet Jacobs, like Frederick Douglass, William Wells Brown, and Harriet Tubman, distinguished between what she believed to be the "right" Christianity and that which characterized her interpretation of southern religion. The Norcoms were members of the church. Yet Jacobs was unimpressed with their tendency to degrade and debase their slaves. Mrs. Norcom never flinched when she witnessed the blood drawn from the continuous blows of the whip and it was not uncommon for her to spit in the meals that the slaves had spent long hours preparing only to demonstrate her power. Dr. Norcom did not fair any better when it came to such matters. If the feast was not up to his standards he would administer a series of lashings upon the cook or induce him or her to digest every last parcel of food while he sat and watched.[13]

The behaviors of the Norcoms and those of the three matriarchs in Harriet's life were equally responsible for shaping her view that there existed a wide irreconcilable chasm between Christianity proper and the practices of slave owners. The theme of holding the master class accountable for their religious misdeeds is found throughout the slave narratives published during the Garrisonian era. Hence, it should come as no surprise that Harriet Jacobs wrote extensively about the lack of moral character she found among the planter class or that she was struck by a more favorable Christianity she later encountered in her travels to England.[14] Even though Harriet Jacobs considered herself a Christian, her religion and the faith of those around her was not without African influences that persisted throughout the antebellum period.

Jacobs identifies some of these African cultural expressions in her discussion of the developments that took place between the slaves of Edenton and the local clergy following the Nat Turner insurrection. Like all black communities, Edenton was adversely affected by the revolt. Suspicions of further conspiracies from both slaves and free blacks ran high and Jacobs recalled witnessing all of the local white men strapping themselves with muskets and ransacking the homes of every black resident shortly after news of the incident spread. Slaves were prohibited from visiting neighboring plantations and worshiping "at their little church in the woods, with their burying ground around it." Appeals to continue their devotions fell on deaf ears and the church which they had built with their own hands and at which they were known to reach their highest state of elation when singing their songs and bursting out into "spontaneous prayer" was destroyed.[15]

Jacobs, in a similar fashion to Frederick Douglass, insisted that the apologists of slavery who argued that the pervasiveness of slave songs throughout the South reflected the humane nature of the peculiar institution were off the mark. She says;

> Precious are such moments to the poor slaves. If you were to hear them at such times, you might think they were happy. But can that hour of singing and shouting sustain them through the dreary week, toiling without wages, under constant dread of the lash?[16]

As the slaves were being forced to abandon their spiritual place of refuge the owners thought it a good idea that they be given "formal" religious instruction to prevent the flourishing of any radical ideas that might have ensued from the Turner rebellion. A local Episcopal clergyman, who Jacobs refers to as Reverend Pike in her narrative, agreed to lead the services. The slaves were hardly receptive to his message of obedience and deference, of which they were encouraged to embrace. Nor did they look favorably upon the Reverend's critique of their African practices when he preached that:

> God sees you. You tell lies. Instead of being engaged in worshipping him, you are hidden away somewhere . . . tossing coffee-grounds with some wicked fortuneteller, or cutting cards with another old hag . . . and tying up little bags of roots to bury under the door-steps to poison each other with . . . you sneak into the back streets, or among the bushes, to pitch coppers.[17]

Though the reverend drew a distinct line between worshipping God and these popular black folk customs, it is unlikely that the congregation perceived such a fine demarcation between their understanding and acknowledgement of a divine presence in their lives and their inclination to consult diviners and engage in the practice of conjuration. In fact those who proved to be proficient diviners and conjure doctors were often believed to be intermediaries between the slaves and the spirit world and were accorded the same level of respect that church goers would have given to a priest or deacon belonging to the Christian clergy.[18] Furthermore, it is probable that the slaves of Edenton participated in these African rituals at the sacred site of their makeshift church which was delineated by their burial grounds since it was here that they found their greatest happiness when singing and creatively improvising their prayers.[19]

Jacobs explained that when Reverend Pike delivered a similar sermon the following Sunday, the slaves eagerly awaited the hour when the service would come to an end so that they could go engage in a ring shout ceremony. She recalled that there were fewer times when the slaves were more blissful than when "shouting and singing at religious meetings" and she was convinced that those who participated in the shout were "nearer to the gate of heaven than sanctimonious Mr. Pike, and other long-faced Christians, who see wounded Samaritans, and pass by on the other side."[20] More so than even her contemporaries Frederick Douglass, William Wells Brown, and Harriet Tubman, all of whom recorded their illuminating observations of or participation in the ring shout, Jacobs, by drawing a connection between the shout and being close to heaven, seems to suggest that she understood that these exercises invoked the presence of ancestors. Religious meetings without the ring shout must have seemed mundane and somewhat pointless not only to Jacobs but to the other slaves who were overcome by excitement when engaged in the ritual—for the shout lay at the core of the slaves' spirituality. It is small wonder then that those who attended the Reverend Pike's meeting had a burning desire to leave so that they could freely shout as they had been accustomed.

It should be noted that Jacobs provides what very well may be the only testimony of the ring shout ceremony in North Carolina and her account confirms that Lydia Parish was incorrect when she concluded that "the ring shout seems to be unknown" in the state.[21] Given the prevalence of African culture throughout the South and even in parts of the North it makes sense that the ring shout was a significant phenomenon in North Carolina, especially since it was here that the African-inspired slave tradition of John Kunering, in which the shout was a major component, was honored, as will become evident further on in this chapter.[22]

The ring shout provided a meeting "space" for the living and the deceased. Few locations, if any, were better to invoke and honor the ancestors through the ring shout than the burial grounds where the slaves often congregated for spiritual reflection and ritual. Slaves grasped in an African sense the significance of the relationship between the living and the dead. In their world, balance and order depended on it. Jacobs believed that the burial grounds were where "the wicked cease from troubling, and there the weary be at rest. There the prisoners rest together; they hear not the voice of the oppressor; the servant is free from his master." It was for this reason that she vowed at the site of her deceased parents to run away from the Norcoms. As Jacobs passed the old dwelling where the slaves worshiped before Nat Turner's revolt she prayed for guidance and protection. Revisiting the grounds reminded her of the numerous times since her mother's death that she seemed to hear her voice "sometimes chiding me, sometimes whispering loving words into my wounded heart." Jacobs does not tell us if this was one of those occasions but she did feel as if she heard her father's voice encouraging her to push forward until she was free. The grounds had never seemed as sacred to Jacobs as they had on this occasion. "My trust in God," she disclosed, "had been strengthened by that prayer among the graves." Perhaps Jacobs also recalled the ring shout ceremonies she had witnessed or even participated in at these burial grounds. What is abundantly clear is that this was a place of sanctity and refuge which was highly regarded by the slaves. [23]

Scholarly attention has been given to the importance of a proper burial ceremony of family members within the slave quarters.[24] When Betty Horniblow, who is identified as Aunt Nancy in Jacobs's narrative, passed away, her mistress Mrs. Norcom (Mrs. Flint) desired to go against the grain of how slaves were typically interred and sought to have her buried in the doctor's family memorial park. Jacobs's grandmother, however, requested that her daughter be laid to rest in the old burying grounds of the slaves and the mistress obliged.[25] Molly Horniblow could not imagine any member of her family being separated in the ancestral realm. The belief that kinship ties should remain intact in the afterlife was not a foreign idea among Africans. In his travels throughout West Africa John Pearce noted that "only relatives may be buried in the same piece of ground together."[26] Though Pearce neglected to inform his interviewers to which region he was referring, such notions were not strange to the Ibo and other African ethnic groups. In his investigation of Nigeria, George Thomas Basden found that it was largely hoped that people "die in their own town or, at least, to be buried within its precincts."[27]

Is it also quite possible that Jacobs's grandmother had reservations about her family being buried with the master class that were similar to those described in the narratives of Frederick Douglass and James W.C. Pennington. Douglass revealed that the slaves of Talbot County Maryland were rather "superstitious" about the slave owner's family burial grounds. Some of the older ones claimed to have seen shrouded spirits that rode on black horses. Others witnessed fire balls and heard strange sounds. All were convinced that slaveholders would be confronted with an ill-fate in their afterlife and these "tales of sights and sounds, strange and terrible, connected with the huge black tombs, were a very great security to the grounds about them, for few of the slaves felt like approaching them even in the day time."[28] Writing in a similar vein of his experience as a slave in Maryland, James W.C. Pennington noted that the blacks had "a superstitious dread of passing the dilapidated dwelling of a man who has been guilty of great cruelties to his slaves, and who is dead, or moved away." Pennington admitted that he was among those who were plagued with this feeling.[29]

Harriet Jacobs believed that "it had never occurred to Mrs. Flint that slaves could have any feelings" about a preference for their final resting place. If Jacobs's mistress had held some sense of what the ring shout ceremony meant she would have at least inferred that the bond that the slaves sought to maintain with their dead was often the cornerstone of their existence. Such a bond could be equally and even more important as that which was forged among the living.

For example, Jacobs's intimate relationship with her parents after they died may have surfaced when she dreamt "strange dreams of the dead and the living" after Betty passed away.[30] On another occasion Jacobs received a vision of her two children when she was sitting by the window listening to the sounds of serenaders who were playing "Home, sweet home." She was well aware that such an experience "reflected the superstition of slaves." The music reminded her of the moaning cries of her children and she witnessed a clear image of them that appeared through a streak of moonlight which reflected off the floor:

> They vanished; but I had seen them distinctly. Some will call it a dream, others a vision. I know not how to account for it, but it made a strong impression on my mind, and I felt certain something had happened to my little ones.[31]

Jacobs' vision was later confirmed when she was informed that her children were sold the previous day to their father and were being looked after by her grandmother. Jacobs attributed this good fortune to none other than divine intervention and she was extremely thankful that her children no longer had to remain with her owner.

We have established in the preceding chapters that slaves took their dreams and visions quite seriously. Jacobs's dreams were no less significant than those of Harriet Tubman who dreamt of John Brown's raid on Harpers Ferry before it occurred or Sandy Jenkins who prophetically dreamt that Frederick Douglass would be apprehended during his first attempt to run away.[32] Jacobs's dream of the living and the deceased provides a rather unique perspective on the intuitive power that gifted slaves claimed to have had. Her clairvoyance in many ways reflects the epitome of slave spirituality. That is that ancestors played a significant role in the governance of one's life.

Jacobs's understanding of the importance of maintaining a relationship with one's ancestors gave her the courage she needed to make the bold step towards freedom and once she gained the confidence she needed to escape, it becomes clear from her account of the initial trials she faced on her journey that she belonged to a slave community that had a keen sense of black folk remedies that were intended to heal illnesses. When Jacobs fled under the cover of darkness she was fortunate to find refuge at the quarters of a nearby friend. Her pursuers were relentless in their efforts to capture her and not long after their search began they had come dangerously close to her hiding place. Jacobs in a state of panic scurried out of her companion's house and concealed herself in a grove of bushes for a couple of hours. While covered by the thick brush a poisonous reptile of some sort bit her leg. She initially tended to her a wound with "a poultice of *warm ashes and vinegar.*" This gave her some relief, but her swelling did not subside. Her friend then "asked an old woman, who doctored among the slaves, what was good for the bite of a snake or a lizard and was told to steep a *dozen coppers in vinegar* to the inflamed part."[33] The reader is led to believe that the prescription worked, for Jacobs gives no indication that the pain failed to subside. Folklorist Newbell Niles Puckett explained that similar remedies could be found among the inhabitants of the Gold Coast: "For a swelling of any sort use mullein tea or a mixture of cream of tartar, *vinegar, and rusty nails* applied as a lotion."[34]

The use of copper-like metals calls to mind Jacob's recollection of Reverend Pike's sermon in which he rebuked the slaves for "sneaking into the back streets, or among the bushes, to pitch coppers." Art historian Robert Farris Thompson points out that bronze was considered a sacred metallic element in the Yoruba pantheon of orisha. Ogun, the deity of war and iron, is often represented through "various expressions of ironwork, such as nails, iron bows and arrows, horseshoes, and fetters."[35] Thus the widespread use of coppers in Edenton appears to have been directly linked to an African appreciation for its metallic properties.

Harriet Jacobs also presents compelling evidence that her family was linked to an African healing tradition in which conjure doctors were thought to have the ability to administer "counter" medicines against "bad magic." After Jacobs had tried her luck with a couple of risky hiding places her family thought it would be wise for her to lodge in the attic of a small shed that was attached to her grandmother's house. Its conditions were of the crudest sort. The highest peak was less than three feet and light and air were scarce. While crawling around on one occasion, as she was accustomed to doing, Jacobs hit her head on a gimlet that was protruding from the door of the attic. This gave her the idea to drill small holes in the wall so that her air supply would increase and that she might catch a glance of her children from time to time. To her discontentment the first passerby Jacobs noticed was Dr. Norcom and she had "a shuddering, superstitious feeling that it was a bad omen." Shortly after this she was plagued "by hundreds of little red insects, fine as a needle's point." Her grandmother prescribed "herb teas and *cooling* medicines" and Jacobs was no longer burdened by the irritants.[36] The belief that the invasion of insects into the body was associated with conjuration was prevalent in coastal Georgia and among the blacks of Suriname and Jacobs's grandmother's remedy of "cooling medicines" was a concept that was understood by the Yoruba speaking peoples of what is now Nigeria.

Charles Singleton of Springfield Georgia recalled a neighbor of his who suffered from crickets crawling under his skin. Singleton attributed the bad fortune to a conjure woman who was known to grind dead insects into a powdery substance and rub the concoction on the victim's skin or put it in their drink. It was his belief that "wen it entuh duh body, it tun back intuh insec, sometime a lizud aw a frawg aw a snake."[37] Writing on the beliefs of the blacks of Suriname, Melville and Frances Herskovits found that *Fiofio* was an insect or spirit that took the shape of an insect that afflicted the human body leading to serious illness and even death. The disease was credited to a family quarreling which was left unresolved.[38]

Molly Horniblow's skill in employing "cooling medicines" to avert the malicious conjure of an insect pestilence resembles the Yoruba concept of *Itutu* that Robert Farris Thompson discusses in *Flash of the Spirit*. Thompson explains that *Itutu* is the concept of "mystic coolness" whereby the literal and figurative meaning of coolness is related to generosity, gentleness, and calmness. *Itutu* was an especially important notion for the artist and the healer. The cool or calm character of the artist allowed for "the critical focus for acts of sacrifice and devotion." It was believed that the gods could be appeased or cooled by offering them cherished objects or conciliatory words. Literal depictions of coolness such as the fanning of a god were not uncommon in Yoruba art.[39] Osanyin, the Yoruba deity of herbalistic medicine that was examined in our treatment of Harriet Tubman, possessed curing powers that were also associated with *tutu* (cool). The colors and cool sparkle of Osanyin's beads were a reflection of various colored healing herbs. More than providing a coolness of aesthetic pleasure, Osanyin's beads were "in a literal sense of referral to leaf like qualities of refreshing taste or smell, and—most important—powers of restoration."[40] Molly Horniblow, like Tubman, had a firm grasp on herbs for their restorative "cooling" purposes in much the same way as the devotees to Osanyin.[41]

Through her reflection of her grandmother it also appears that Harriet Jacobs, like Tubman, had a grasp on the notion of the "flying African."[42] Jacobs explains that her painful memories of slavery were softened by tender recollections of her "good old grandmother, like light, fleecy clouds floating over a dark troubled sea."[43] Karen Beardslee effectively makes the case that Jacobs's metaphorical imagery of her grandmother floating like a cloud calls to mind the African belief that ancestors were intimately involved with the living.[44] Beardslee's analysis can be taken a step further when Jacobs's account of her grandmother, who in many ways resembled Harriet Tubman as a spiritual matriarch and conjure doctor, is considered alongside Tubman's dream of flying over fields and towns, and rivers and mountains prior to her escape to the North. Molly's flight over the dark troubled sea represented her difficult life while Tubman in her dream soared over the south which held many of the same troubles that Molly encountered.[45]

Harriet Jacobs's most intriguing remarks on the persistence of African culture within the slave quarters were of the annual John Kunering parade in North Carolina. The festival was a sort of carnival which coincided with the Christmas season and usually lasted until the New Year. Its central features included circular dance, improvisational singing,

African instrumentation, brightly colored garb, a stick or whip designed to keep onlookers at a distance and masks which sometimes took the form of houseboats or canoes.[46]

The center of the Kuner festival was in Wilmington, North Carolina and extended to the towns of Edenton, New Bern, Hillsboro, Hilton, Fayetteville and Southport.[47] Jacobs offers what very well may be the finest description of the festival from the vantage point of the slave as she observed it each year in Edenton:

> Every child rises early on Christmas morning to see the Johnkannaus. Without them, Christmas would be shorn of its greatest attraction. They consist of companies of slaves from the plantations, generally of the lower class. Two athletic men, in calico wrappers, have a *net thrown* over them, covered with all manner of bright-colored stripes. Cows' tails are fastened to their backs, and their heads are decorated with horns. A box, covered with sheepskin, is called the gumbo box. A dozen beat on this, while others strike triangles and jawbones, to which bands of dancers keep time. For a month previous they are composing songs, which are sung on this occasion. These companies, of a hundred each, turn out early in the morning, and are allowed to go round till twelve o'clock, begging for contributions.[48]

Ira Reid has identified a number of North Carolinian pronunciations and spellings for the festival that were used interchangeably including *John Kooner, John Kuner, John Canoe, Who-Who's,* and *Joncooner.*[49] Given the Caribbean's early contributions of slaves to British North America it is not altogether surprising that Jacobs's appropriation of the festival as *Johnkannaus* is closest to one of the West Indian versions *Junkanoes.*[50] For the purpose of uniformity the spelling *John Kuner* is employed here.

Much of the description that Sterling Stuckey unearthed from a Dr. Edward Warren who frequented the Collins estate in the first half of the nineteenth century in Washington County, North Carolina and witnessed slaves engaging in the John Kunering ceremony mirrors Jacobs's account. Collins also found that two men were the focal point of the ceremony. The costume of the individual leading the procession who was known as the "ragman" consisted of loose and dangling "rags." The head adornments, which according to Stuckey symbolized the presence of ancestors, were comprised of "two great ox horns." The second character known as the "Number Two" was responsible for collecting the presents in a small cup or bowl. Cow or sheep bells were draped over the participant's shoulders for the purpose of producing a jingle-like effect during the ceremony. Warren also mentioned wooden "gumba boxes," that were "covered over with tanned sheep-skins".[51] The beating of the gumba boxes signaled the procession towards the great house. The "ragman" and the "number two" then led the parade in a dance of the most extraordinary improvisation.

The latter danced his way towards the master requesting a token for his talents. The climax of the dancing ceremony was the ring shout.[52] Thus, those slaves in Edenton who eagerly awaited the opportunity to engage in the ring shout would have been among those anxiously anticipating the parade.

Stuckey establishes compelling connections between John Kuner and similar affairs that took place in Nigeria. He directs us to the findings of Amaury Talbot who observed the harvest festival known as Ikunle. Its purpose was to honor the ancestors who founded towns. As Jacobs described in Kunering, those who participated in Ikunle wore nets or wooden masks over their faces as they danced through the streets. An integral element of Ikunle that was also found in Kunering was of long wands or sticks designed to keep bystanders at bay. Talbot also wrote of an Egun ceremony that bears remarkable similarities with the Christmas tradition of gift giving. This might have served as a great source of reinforcement for African practices through Christmas celebrations.[53] Another example of masking ceremonies comes from Sierra Leone where the elaborate costumes were similar to those described by Jacobs.[54]

While various forms of Kunering have also been documented in Jamaica, Cuba, and the Bahamas, the consensus among scholars is that the revelry surrounding the festival which Jacobs so impressively described did not extend beyond North Carolina in the United States.[55] Yet, when Jacobs' account is read alongside the narratives of Jacob Stroyer and Charles Ball it appears that some semblance of the festival was not unfamiliar to South Carolinian slaves.

Stroyer recalled that when South Carolinian slaveholders yielded a good harvest during the Christmas season the slaves were allowed to stop working from five to six days. Those who were born in Africa "would sing some of their songs, or tell different stories of the customs in Africa. After this they would spend half a day dancing in some large cotton house or on a scaffold." Fiddlers served as the instruments of choice. The best dancers received gifts of tobacco, hats, and handkerchiefs. Monetary rewards generally amounted between fifteen to twenty dollars.[56] Stroyer's account is strikingly similar to both the Ikunle harvest festival and the Egun ceremony of gift giving. In Sterling Stuckey's discussion of the "Bur Rabbit and Red Hill Churchyard" tale collected in South Carolina by E.C.L. Adams, he sheds light on the incorporation the fiddle. Stuckey concluded that Brer Rabbit used the fiddle in the same way some of the Akan speakers used the drum. It was believed that the instruments had the power to summon the ancestors, communicate with them and send them back to world of the spirits—a process that would have not been foreign to those taking part in John Kuner.[57]

In Charles Ball's slave narrative the author also remembered the singing, dancing, and playing of the banjo that accompanied the stories that African-born slaves told of their homeland in South Carolina.[58] His account of an African gentleman who buried his infant son may be linked to the John

Kuner festival and might provide clues on what the linguistic appropriation of "Kuner" to "canoe" actually meant for the slaves. The child died just a few days before Christmas and was buried with "a small bow and several arrows; a little bag of parched meal; a miniature canoe, about a foot long, and a little paddle, (with which he said it would cross the ocean to his own country) a small stick, with an iron nail, sharpened, and fastened into one end of it; and a piece of white muslin," with several brightly colored figures painted on it.[59]

Robert Smith in his investigation of the canoe in pre-colonial West Africa contends that the vessel was vital to trading, fishing, and warfare pursuits across the region. From the pre-colonial era through the twentieth century the builders of canoes were considered specialists who often based their designs on "'children's boats' sent to them as models" and it is possible the burial ceremony that Ball witnessed in which a miniature canoe was buried with the child was related to this custom.[60] The arrows that were included with the corpse can be explained by the numerous accounts of war fleets consisting of canoes from the sixteenth century on that were equipped with weapons that included arrows.[61] There is also a link between spears and other weapons in warring canoes and the sticks or long wands that were used in Kuner festivals. Balls's description of the bright colored paintings parallels Jacobs's account of the bright colored stripes that adorned the two athletic men in calico wrappers. Because the burial ceremony took place during the Christmas season when John Kuner usually occurred strengthens the likelihood that some of these items were indeed symbols of the festival.

Replicas of canoes were essential features in a number of Kunering festivals. Reid suggests that the appearance of the canoe or houseboat is conclusively connected with English mummery festivals where a number of the mummers wore ship-like headdresses.[62] Though there has not been a discussion on whether or not the slaves brought new meaning to the canoe, what Robert Smith has to tell us of 'canoe houses' in the eastern Niger region may shed further light on the festival's African influences. He writes: "Society came to be organized around the canoes in 'canoe houses', which replaced the traditional houses based on ties of blood. The canoe house has been described as 'a compact and well organized trading and fighting corporation, capable of manning and maintaining a war canoe." These canoe 'houses' had become so popular in the late eighteenth and early nineteenth centuries that they were "the very basis of the state."[63]

Some of the Kuner songs can provide further clues as to what the incorporation of the canoe meant to the slaves. As was the case with a number of slave spirituals, the underlying message of these songs was escape. When slaves felt that they had not received a large enough reward they sang:

> "Run, Jinnie, run! I'm gwine away,
> Bwine away, to come no mo'.

Dis am de po' house.
Glory Habbilulum!
Hah! Low! Here we go!
Hah! Low! Here we go!
Hah! Low! Kuners comin'[64]

Another song incorporated call and response, thus giving it the same effect as negro work and camp meeting songs:

Solo: Young gal go ROUND de Corner!
Chorus in harmony: My true love gone DOWN de lane!
Solo: Wet on de grass where de djew been poured.
Chorus: Hey, me lady, go DOWN de road; Go Down de road; go DOWN de road! My true love gone DOWN de lane.[65]

Other Kuners sang

> She stood long on the shore
> Eyes grow dim with tears
> Oh I lak to melt
> She went across the seas
> She swung a kiss to me
> I'll wait for her
> I'll be true to her
> As de skies above
> I'll awit my darlin' girl.[66]

A village tailor from Lacovia, Jamaica, revealed he led a company of actors who performed an annual play during the Kunering season in which the first line was "I wonder how the king escape! Heaven knows."[67]

It was not uncommon for slaves to draw on the Igbo notion of returning back to Africa through flight. It is quite possible that the canoe used in Kunering festivals represented another intended means to accomplish this.[68] The short stick and the brightly colored muslin cloth or rags that were buried with the African's son would have not been unfamiliar items to Kuners. It is safe to conclude that the record that Michael Gomez came across in which Georgia slaves from Hutchinson Island set out in a canoe with three paddles with the intention of returning home was not an isolated incident. While their preferred route was water as opposed to air they shared the same goals as the Igbo and given the prevalence of canoes in West Africa we can assume that there were several more.[69]

Peter Gutkind in his article *The Canoemen of the Gold Coast (Ghana)* examines the working class consciousness that developed among this occupational group. Beginning in the eighteenth century those who manned canoes became increasingly fearful of being sold into slavery and records indicate that many ran away. There were also persons who simply refused to work and others who demanded greater subsistence for their labor—a concept to which Kuners easily related.[70] The Kunering practice of performing for monetary rewards was not strange to the canoemen of the Gold Coast. Visitors often noted their songs "and their pleading for a 'dashee' (tip)."[71] Slaves whose lineage was linked to the Gold Coast may have also found inspiration for the incorporation of brightly colored cloth that was used in Kunering festivals from their homeland. Gutkind charges that there was a close relationship between the *asafo*, a military organization of the region, and the canoemen. Each *asafo* unit laid claim to "distinct emblems and flags, which, annually, continue to be paraded." On occasion the parades became affairs of civil disturbance "directed against chiefs and the introduction of direct taxation."[72] Hence, slaves could have drawn from ample African models for their connection to canoes and or 'houseboats' and the ideologies of a working class consciousness that were associated with the festival. It is fair to say that Jacobs's reflections of Kunering and the ring shout alone designate her as one of the most astute observers and transcribers of slave culture. For her, the festival was very much a family affair. Even her grandmother played an instrumental role during the Kunering season. "Grandmother brought me materials," Jacobs says "and I busied myself making some new garments and little playthings for my children."[73]

Molly Horniblow was the bedrock of Jacobs's family and she served as a constant reinforcement of African values. Like Frederick Douglass's grandmother, who was held in high regard for her agricultural, fishing and midwifery skills, Molly was accorded a similar esteem as "she had for a long time supplied many families with crackers and preserves; consequently, 'Aunt Marthy,' as she was called, was generally known, and every body who knew her respected her intelligence and good character."[74] Given what Douglass tells us about the use of "uncle" to refer to elder slaves who were proficient in certain skills and William Wells Brown's account of senior conjure doctors who were also called "uncle," it makes sense that Jacobs's grandmother who knew how to cure ailments and was a master baker was called "Aunt Marthy." As argued in our fuller discussion of Douglass, such manners strengthened African values and kinship associations in America.[75]

Jacobs and her grandmother, as Jean Yellin has pointed out, challenged the contemporary social structure of the dominant patriarchy that perpetuated a culture of gender inequality.[76] Jacobs overcame the sexual abuse of Dr. Norcom and her grandmother was able to carve out a position of relative power by maintaining a close relationship with influential whites and functioning as a matriarchal figure for the local slaves and free blacks. She managed all of the household duties from wet nursing and preparing the meals to sewing the clothes with such shrewdness "that her master and mistress could not help seeing it was for their interest to take care of such a valuable piece of property."[77] Molly Horniblow was not afraid to speak her mind. When Dr. Norcom struck Jacobs on one occasion in Molly's house the "good grandmother" demanded that the doctor leave her residence immediately and warned that since he did not have many more years to live he would be wise to pray to purge his tarnished soul. Though upset, the doctor heeded her demand and left the house. Even as a slave she held some power.[78]

Jacobs believed that she too possessed the vigor to control her fate. She manipulated Dr. Norcom through her deceptive escape and she was convinced that her strong commitment to her children alone was a comparable "weapon" to her master's tyranny. "My master had power and law on his side," she writes "I had a determined will. There is might in each."[79] When her son Joseph, who is identified as Benny in the narrative, was just twelve years old he also was quite capable of exerting what little power he could over Dr. Norcom. Joseph had become suspicious of his mother's hiding place early on and thus strived to keep his playmates away from that side of the house. He maintained a close eye on Dr. Norcom's comings and goings and whenever he overheard him conversing with the local patrollers he relayed the information to his great grandmother.[80] Even at this young age Joseph was keenly aware of the lack of protection that was afforded the slave. He knew that only measures taken by the family matriarch could potentially ensure his mother's true security.

Joseph was subscribing to family values that were passed on from generation to generation. Their father Elijah sought to instill similar principles in Jacobs and her brother John. Jacobs recalled the occasion when her brother, after having been called by their father and mistress at the same time, responded to his mistress. Disturbed by his son's insubordination, Elijah chastised "you are my child and when I call you, you should come immediately, if you have to pass through fire and water."[81] The notion that slavery was a kind-loving paternal order made little sense to Jacobs and it was no less a peculiar concept to the rest of her family.

While Jacobs attested to the kindness of her first mistress for teaching her to read and treating her with some degree of humanity, she never lost sight that she was a slave owner who failed to free her in her will as she had promised she would.[82] Jacobs agreed with her contemporaries Frederick Douglass, William Wells Brown, and other abolitionists on the subject of plantation paternalism. In her view, the Reverend Nehemiah Adams's *A South-Side View of Slavery* (1854) wrongly concluded that slavery was a benign and patriarchal institution in which slaves expressed no desire to be free. He attributed this view to nothing less than a facade staged by slaveholders for the purpose of convincing northern visitors who were ignorant of southern slavery that slaves were not devoid of material or social comforts.[83] Jacobs felt that had northerners spent any considerable amount of time in the south they would have witnessed such atrocities as starving laborers toiling from sunup to sundown, cries from mothers separated from their offspring, the sexual exploitation of young girls, the all too frequent occurrence of dog-catchers trained to feast on slave flesh, and "pools of blood around the whipping post."[84]

Jacobs was first introduced to northern abolitionists shortly after she escaped from Edenton in the early 1840s. Yet, it was not until she moved from Boston to Rochester in March of 1849 to be closer to her daughter who was attending boarding school in the area and her brother John who was carving out his place as an up and coming agent for the anti-slavery society that she began to develop a close relationship with those involved in the movement.[85] John managed the Rochester Anti-slavery Reading Room and went on the lecture circuit with Fredrick Douglass to promote *The North Star.* While John was touring Jacobs worked at the reading room and cultivated a close relationship with his abolitionist friends Amy and Isaac Post who were fairly popular in Garrisonian circles. Jacobs ended up living with the Posts and became quite familiar with the work that Amy was doing with the Seneca Fall's Woman's Rights Convention.

Jean Yellin claims that it was during her time among the Posts that the roots of Jacobs's later relief work with refugees in Virginia, D.C., and Savannah were planted. Jacobs shared a familial intimacy with her hosts and eventually felt comfortable enough to impart her story to Amy who in-turn convinced her to tell it to the world. Yellin suggests that though Amy was just ten years Jacobs's senior, Jacobs's may have looked towards her as sort of mother figure who reminded her of Molly Horniblow. This idea is even more plausible when the spiritual experiences of the Posts are taken into account. Yellin reveals that they regularly participated in séances or "scientific demonstrations." Those engaged in such episodes claimed to have had the ability to act as spiritual mediums whereby they could contact people who were not in their immediate vicinity or those who had passed away.[86] Since Jacobs claimed to have communicated with her parents after they died, had visions of her children and understood how important it was for her grandmother to have her family interred at the slave burial grounds, the séances Jacobs witnessed from the Posts may have been a critical bridge in their relationship.

The work of Yellin and those scholars following in her footsteps is bringing Harriet Jacobs back to the forefront of American memory. Yellin is currently editor of the Harriet Jacobs Papers Project which promises to be a watershed in the historiographical and literary tradition of American slavery. It will be the first time that letters and other pertinent documents from a slave woman are compiled into a published volume and it may provide further evidence of the cultural memory that Jacobs exhibits in *Incidents.*

5 Discourse on the Slave Narrative and a New Interpretation of Black Anti-Slavery Ideology

When U. B. Phillips wrote *Life and Labor in the Old South* (1929) he argued that slave narratives should not be considered worthy sources for historical inquiry because they were imbued with too much abolitionist editing and rhetoric.[1] Taking the lead from antebellum southern apologists of slavery who proclaimed that these texts were little more than gross fabrications, Phillips discouraged his contemporaries from chronicling or drawing on a genre whose authenticity he believed to be questionable. This was the general consensus among scholars until Benjamin A. Botkin, the chief Librarian for the Library of Congress, released the Federal Writers Project (FWP) slave narrative collection in 1944. Botkin's decision to grant public access to twenty-five hundred oral interviews conducted by former slaves in seventeen states sparked a renewed interest in slave testimonies.[2]

Marion Starling's 1946 dissertation, "The Slave Narrative: Its Place in American Literary History," was a product of this reinvigorated intellectual curiosity and it marked a turning point in studies on the slave narrative as she was the first student of slavery to amass a large repository of authentic slave narratives up until that time. Though Starling chose not to publish her manuscript until 1981 for personal reasons, historian John Blassingame credited her dissertation with inaugurating "the modern era of Afro-American historical writing with its focus on giving a voice to the oppressed."[3] Starling found that narratives published prior to the Garrisonian abolitionist movement during the eighteenth and early nineteenth centuries tended to have an underlying theme of adventure that focused on the authors' individual escapes. She concluded that the texts appearing after 1836, which reflected a moral and economic class consciousness connected to the new anti-slavery movement, called for an immediate rather than the gradual end to slavery that was espoused by abolitionists of the late eighteenth century.[4] That Starling had just received her Ph.D. in English with a minor in history from New York University may have made historians reluctant to see the value in her research. Few heeded the call to examine the documents and those who did remained suspicious.

While Kenneth Stampp in his study *The Peculiar Institution: Slavery in the Ante-Bellum South* (1956) made use of the narratives of Solomon

Northup, Frederick Douglass, William Wells Brown, Austin Steward, and Jermain W. Lougen to cite examples of slave labor patterns, their Christian influences, the nature of their treatment, and to conclude that slaves were unable to forge a social milieu of their own, he was convinced that most of the narratives that were resurfacing in the 1940s were unreliable and concluded that "one can only infer their thoughts and feelings from their behavior, that of their masters, and the logic of their situation."[5] Historian Stanley Elkins, in his book *Slavery: A Problem in American Institutional and Intellectual Life*, also reasons that the genre was of little value to scholars interested in slavery and does not treat a single narrative. In a footnote in which he discusses the importance of sources, Elkins argues that the eyewitness accounts of whites such as Nehemiah Adams and Frederika Bremer are more insightful than the accounts located in slave narratives, but he does not demonstrate why such might be the case. Elkins insists that only the narratives of ex-slaves Solomon Northup and Peter Still offer accurate portrayals of southern life. He proclaims that "Frederick Douglass' *My Bondage and My Freedom* is obviously not the work of an ordinary slave, but some of the author's insights into the slave system are very valuable." Though Elkins may have recognized the increasing fascination with slave narratives and thus felt the need to at least mention them in a footnote, he did not refer to them anywhere else in his investigation.[6]

In *Puttin' on ole massa; the Slave Narratives of Henry Bibb, William Wells Brown and Solomon Northup* (1969) historian Gilbert Osofsky not only challenges Elkins's theory that slaves were prone to look towards the master class for models of behavior and authority, he was among the first scholars to refute U.B. Phillips's notion that slave narratives were illegitimate sources. Osofsky explains that the anti-slavery press prevented most false accounts from slipping through the cracks by frequently warning their readers of the forged accounts that did surface. Seeking to quell the proliferation of bogus accounts, editors and publishers carefully scrutinized potential memoirs and implemented a strict process of verifying the accuracy of one's story.[7] Since Osofsky accepted the narratives as a window into the private mind of the slave he drew different conclusions than Elkins. His close reading of Bibb, Wells Brown, Northup, and others gave him the impression that rather than locating paternal figures in their owners, slaves drew their values from other slave authority figures who served their community as preachers, storytellers, and local healers versed in root medicine and capable of interpreting dreams.[8] Osofsky ultimately conceded that European and African cultures were equally influential in the slave community. His inclusion of the African background cut against the grain of what most scholars were arguing at that time. He quite convincingly suggests that the slaves' incorporation of the devil, "Old Sam," into their texts reflects a syncretic influence of the Old Testament spirit and an African folk hero such as Anansi the spider, the Afro-Brazilian deity Exu, or the Haitian deity Legba. It was believed that these divinities had the tragic or comical ability to manipulate one's fate and for this reason must be appeased. Osofsky directs us to an amusing slave song that William Wells Brown documented that was rooted in these ideas:

> If de Debble do not ketch
> Jeff. Davis, dat infernal retch,
> An roast and frigazee dat rebble,
> Wat is de use of any Debble?[9]

Henry Bibb's narrative, too, caught the attention of Osofsky. He explained that Bibb's description of a toad as a love charm mirrors Afro-Brazilian rites of "sexual magic."[10] Osofsky urged students of slavery to consider the folkloric value of the narratives. But few heeded the call. If scholars had, there would have likely been more studies during this period that expanded upon Osofsky's brief yet significant discussion of African folk ways that made their way into the narratives.

We know from Arna Bontemps's seminal historical novel *Black Thunder* (1968) that he was certainly capable of offering this sort of cultural analysis. In his introduction to *Great Slave Narratives*, Bontemps notes that slaves drew on the oral tradition of their African ancestors "and created folk music, the spirituals, and adapted to their new situation the folk tales from Africa." [11] Yet he says little more about African influences. Perceptive scholar of folklore that he was, if Bontemps had decided to provide a more extensive critical assessment of the genre it is likely that he would have delved deeply into African cultural elements. Bontemps did, like a number of literary critics in the following decade, recognize the influence that slave narratives had on subsequent writings of the twentieth century. "Certainly neither Mark Twain nor Herman Melville escaped its influence completely," he writes "and writing by black authors from James Weldon Johnson to Richard Wright, Ralph Ellison, and James Baldwin shows a profound indebtedness to this tradition."[12]

In 1972 historian Eugene Genovese authored what some considered up until that time the most comprehensive study on slavery—*Roll, Jordan, Roll: The World the Slaves Made*. To support his argument that slaves more often than not encountered kind, altruistic paternal masters, Genovese relied heavily on the Federal Writers' Project (FWP) slave interviews collected during the 1930s and to a lesser extent on writings published during the nineteenth century.[13] If Genovese had provided a more even treatment of the narratives and critically considered the methods employed by the FWP interviewers he may have drawn different conclusions. John Blassingame wrote two groundbreaking books in the 70s that did just that. *The Slave Community: Plantation Life in the Antebellum South* appeared the same year as Genovese's study and was revised in 1979. Blassingame made extensive use of the full length book narratives of the nineteenth century and effectively demonstrated that the arguments put forth by

Southern romantics who claimed that slavery was a benign institution were unfounded. According to Blassingame, one need only to comb through the memoirs of former slaves and consider them against the corresponding evidence found in antebellum court records, newspapers, memoirs and plantation diaries to learn of the inhumane nature of the slave system.[14]

In the introduction to his edited volume *Slave Testimony* (1977), a comprehensive collection of primary source including letters, speeches, interviews, and autobiographies, he expands upon *The Slave Community*. Blassingame advances Gilbert Osofsky's claim that slave narratives were for the most part a reliable body of literature. He demonstrates that most of the editors and amanuenses were employed in other professions where deciphering truth from fiction would not have been uncommon. Several worked as lawyers, scientists, teachers, historians, journalists, ministers, and physicians and when the few narratives written by imposters did appear, the editors, fearing a backlash from pro-slavery advocates, earnestly sought to put a stop these fraudulent accounts.[15]

Blassingame also reiterates the point he made in his first book that there were problems with naively accepting the FWP interviews on face value. He stresses that the failure to lend an uncritical eye to these records can lead to the erroneous conclusion that slavery was a paternalistic institution in which mutual love and admiration between slaves and their masters was the norm.[16]

Given the contemporary racial climate, there was a tendency for southern white interviewers to omit responses of ex-slaves that ran counter to the paternalistic portrait they sought to paint. During the first half of the 1930s the number of black lynchings in the South were soaring and many blacks were burdened with overwhelming debt, discriminatory labor contracts, and limitations on their travel. In effect then, there was pressure to provide the "right" answers to questions concerning the kindness of the master class. Blassingame also points out that there was a significant age discrepancy between the authors of the more extensive narratives of the eighteenth and nineteenth centuries and the interviewees of the 1930s. Authors of the full length autobiographies had an average age of fifty-two years, while the large majority of the later accounts came from persons who were at least eighty years of age. Despite Blassingame's caveats, he ultimately concedes that there is much value in the twentieth-century interviews. While their brevity distorts the image of the slave personality beyond their childhood years, the accounts contain descriptions of a slave culture similar to those found in their speeches, letters, interviews, and autobiographies from the eighteenth and nineteenth centuries.[17]

Blassingame actually offers similar interpretations of the slaves' cultural influences to those put forth by Genovese. Yet, since this was not the central focus of their studies, they, like Gilbert Osofsky, did not provide an extensive treatment on the subject. Nevertheless, what they do have to say is insightful. Genovese cites the narratives of William Wells Brown,

Frederick Douglass and some of the FWP interviews for his discussion on the prevalence of conjurers and fortunetellers within the slave quarters. However, Brown and Douglass are the only authors he utilizes for his discussion on African culture.[18] In his chapter "Enslavement, Acculturation, and African Survivals" in *The Slave Community*, Blassingame examines Douglass's commentary on linguistic survivals and Charles Ball's revelations on the persistence of Islam and African burial rites. Blassingame briefly mentions that the narratives of Jacob Stroyer, John Brown, and Austin Steward, too, include telling accounts of African culture.[19] Though he does not rely heavily on these sources to corroborate his conclusions on African culture, Blassingame's book was the first comprehensive historical study entirely devoted to slave autobiographies and it helped to pave the way for subsequent studies on slave culture.

1972 also marked the year that Marxist historian and sociologist George P. Rawick made a significant contribution to scholarship on the slave narratives in the forty-one volume series *The American Slave: A Composite Autobiography* which amassed the FWP interviews of the 1930s.[20] His introduction to the volume *From Sundown to Sunup: The Making of the Black Community* reflected his longstanding activism and interdisciplinary background as well as his desire to see the contemporary movement of the *Left* abandon its paternalistic attitude towards the black leadership of the Civil Rights Movement.[21] He wrote a history from the bottom up whereby slaves were depicted as the leaders of the abolitionist movement and functioned as the primary actors through the Civil War and Reconstruction periods. He reasons that:

> If America is to be mankind's last, best hope, it will be because there will be found ways of releasing the creative and revolutionary force of the American people. The black community will be in the forefront of those changes if they occur. This is the promise and the challenge of the development of the American black community from 1619 to the present—a community which has always taken the lead in the struggle for the realization of the promise of the Declaration of Independence.[22]

Rawick, like Osofsky and Blassingame, repudiated Stanley Elkins's argument that the infantile docile prototype he referred to as *Sambo* was pervasive throughout the slave quarters. Rather, Rawick concluded that slaves forged their own communities, maintained strong familial bonds of extended kinship ties, and engaged in acts of small scale resistance by drawing on African values and infusing their cultural memory with the social norms of Europeans that they had encountered in America.[23] Rawick, however, did not draw extensively on the interviews he was introducing and many of his conclusions were undocumented.[24] Nonetheless, the true value of his work lies in his bringing a great many narratives together in his volume. Up until that time scholars were limited in their ability to procure the interviews which were housed at the Rare Books Division of the Library of Congress.

Two years following the publications of Genovese, Blassingame, and Rawick, literary critic Stephen Butterfield, in his book *Black Autobiography in America* (1974) devoted the first section of his study to "The Slave-Narrative Period" which he delineates from 1831–1895. Butterfield argues that the preponderance of the texts are permeated with a fierce Christian sentiment responsible for bringing a sense of coherency to the ex-slave's existence. Butterfield reads this religious expression and evidence of other cultural values contained throughout the texts as magnified imitative representations of white cultural norms. He concludes that slave narratives contain expressions of religion, the spirit of freedom, and overall experiences that are identical to those found in Puritan autobiographies. Authors drew on principles particular to whites, he asserts, because the ex-slaves sought to appease those who comprised the majority of their readership. Butterfield charges that since the primary goals of the authors was to rouse support for the anti-slavery cause, there was seldom any need to include African forms and motifs in the texts which would only serve to thwart the notion that blacks were capable of becoming whole human beings in the eyes of whites.[25]

The influence of Puritan values on the writers tells only part of the story. Rather than viewing William Wells Brown's description of a slave woman who while unchained on board a slave trading vessel sought to save her soul by jumping off the boat as an African cultural folk articulation of flight, Butterfield reasons that Wells Brown was simply mimicking the slaveholder's concern of economic loss when he informs the reader that "cases have occurred in which slaves have got off their chains, and made their escape at landing-places, while the boats were taking in wood." Butterfield characterizes Brown's final statement on the matter as the ultimate "understatement" or "significant silence" when he again echoes the attitude of the slaveholders' monetary burden, "she was not chained."[26] Yet Brown was anything but reticent. He suggests that this act of freedom through death was not an isolated incident. Furthermore, he explains that this particular woman could not bear the thought of being separated from her husband and children and "in the agony of her soul jumped overboard, and drowned herself."[27]

It has been said throughout this investigation that the African notion of seeking a sort of spiritual refugee through flight was not uncommon in the South. That Brown did not make an explicit association between suicide and African values and may have been unaware that such a connection existed does not necessarily undermine the African cultural insight of his observations. Moreover, contrary to Butterfield's conclusion, Brown or any other slave would not have had to embrace the mentality of the slaveholder to recognize the economic value that they had to their owners.

Butterfield provides a similar interpretation of Nat Turner's narrative. He contends that the religious mysticism that Turner experienced when he spent time alone in the wilderness is a theme that runs throughout Puritan autobiography. Referring to the writings of Puritans Cotton Mather and John Edwards who expressed a personal and tangible relationship with God, faith in witchcraft, the reading of nature's signs to interpret God's will, and the belief in apocalyptic visions, Butterfield argues that Turner's confessions of his stint in the woods serves as a historical and literary counterpoint to the Puritan tradition. Turner also had visions, associated the signs of nature with prophetic messages from God and conveyed a belief in the supernatural. Butterfield discusses at length how Turner imparts "the most explicit example of any of the slave narratives of Christian rhetoric and imagery which is adapted to the needs of the slave." While Butterfield postulates that Turner may have also been drawing on African influences he does not expand on the matter.[28] He accurately notes that the narratives of Henry Bibb, James W.C. Pennington, and other ex-slaves demonstrate that the authors' process of learning to read and write was a means to realizing their identity as devout Christians. However, Butterfield again says nothing of their African influences.[29]

Robert Stepto's *From Behind the Veil: A Study of Afro-American Narrative* (1979) also examines the slave narrative. Stepto set out to classify what he viewed as the four literary forms that comprised the narrative and the related twentieth-century black autobiographies. These included the *eclectic*, *integrated*, *generic,* and *authenticating* phases of narration. According to Stepto, the phase determined the extent to which the authors had control over their voice. The *eclectic* phase embodies what Stepto terms the "basic" slave narrative. The authors clustered in this category exhibit considerably less control than their editors who take great liberty in deciding what and how many authenticating documents (records from reputable whites that vouch for the author's legitimacy) are included in the text. According to Stepto, Henry Bibb's narrative is the classic example of the *eclectic* form. Lucius Matlack, the editor of the text, wrote the introduction and selected additional authenticating documents with the intention of convincing the white readership that the account was a legitimate testimony produced by a literate Bibb. Stepto argues that Bibb's disconnectedness from Matlack's introduction and the other authenticating documents afforded him less authoritative control and ironically rendered him only somewhat literate.[30]

Stepto identifies the *integrated* form, the second phase of authentication, as a more advanced phase whereby the authors have more freedom to tell their story by incorporating the authenticating documents into the text. Through this process the author is able to speak with a single voice as he or she in the body of the narrative recalls those people who their reading audience would embrace as trustworthy endorsers, rather than appending authenticating documents. This phase is best exemplified by the narrative of Solomon Northup. Though Northup does not have complete control over his narrative because he still includes some supplemental documents in the appendix, he was more involved in the decision making process than Henry Bibb.[31]

The *generic* narratives are more sophisticated than those falling under the *integrated* phase and writing in this vein is Frederick Douglass. While Douglass adds authenticating documents to his narrative, they do not muffle his voice. He exhibits considerable control and becomes a participant observer through his ability to engage a multitude of writing styles. Douglass does not simply record his story. He offers the reader a rich reflective analysis of his life and through this process presents a more complete narrative.[32] The final phase of narration, the *authenticating* form, occurs when an author, like William Wells Brown, is able to make the text an authenticating document for other generic narratives. For example, Brown as a historian, novelist, and playwright shapes his own authenticating strategies by deciding what documents to insert, including his own.[33]

The second half of Stepto's study considers the ways in which some of the twentieth-century black canonical texts not only make use of the various authenticating strategies employed by the authors of slave narratives, but also echo and recast particular literary tropes found in the earlier texts.[34] In Stepto's discussion of how James Weldon Johnson in his *Autobiography of an Ex-Coloured Man* drew on the slave narrative legacy of the snug cottage located in the writings of Harriet Jacobs and Henry Bibb, he misses an opportunity to explore the relationship between the theme of African culture that first appears in the slave narratives and how it continued to receive attention from black authors of the twentieth century.

Stepto calls attention to the Ex-Coloured Man's description of his childhood home in Georgia and maintains that his description of the house and its inhabitants are in many ways a reconstruction of the relations between masters and slaves. It was also at this dwelling that the author encountered flowers that "grew in the front yard, and that around each bed of flowers was a hedge of various coloured glass bottles stuck in the ground neck down." The Ex-Coloured Man never forgot his mother's reproach when his curiosity of whether or not the bottles grew like the flowers had prompted him to excavate the peculiar objects. Drawing on conversations he had with Art historian Robert Farris Thompson, Stepto acknowledges that the adornment of multi-colored bottles is an expression of African culture incorporating the belief that the spirit of one's ancestors can be "captured" and honored through reflective objects. This practice was particularly common in Kongo cosmology. While Stepto crafts a compelling and innovative analysis, he is less concerned with how the text serves as a record of African continuities than he is with the Ex-Coloured Man's failure to embrace or understand this aspect of his African heritage. Since African culture was often expressed beyond the purview of the master class, it should be among the determining factors in assessing the degree to which authors had control over their texts. Moreover, an examination of African culture in the writings of twentieth-century blacks can shed additional light on the correlation between the texts of both periods.[35]

Trailing the footsteps of Stepto's study was John Sekora and Darwin Turner's edited work *The Art of Slave Narrative: Original Essays in Criticism and Theory* (1982). The contributors to the volume who devoted particular attention to how the texts can be used as cultural lenses shared the general consensus that the authors and editors of slave narratives were compelled to present a slave community that was heavily acculturated into white society. Similarly, literary critic William Andrews's essay "The First Fifty Years of the Slave Narrative, 1760–1810" addresses the overwhelming control that editors and amanuenses had over the texts. Andrews charges that this control prevented the authors of early narratives from presenting personal accounts that went beyond the construction of the Judeo-Christian literary and cultural tradition. According to him, the early slave narratives, such as those authored by Britton Hammon, James Gronniosaw, Venture Smith, George White, and Olaudah Equiano lacked the African-American vein of W.E.B. DuBois's concept of double consciousness. Andrews maintains that the texts highlight a single culture reflective of white society.[36]

Annette Niemtzow's essay "The Problematic Self in Autobiography" posits a similar analysis for the narratives of Frederick Douglass and Harriet Jacobs. Niemtzow proclaims that Douglass adopts a white definition of selfhood by drawing on the structures of white autobiography and white culture. She reasons that Douglass strives to legitimize his own self by adhering to the requisite autobiographical patterns of parental heritage. In Niemtzow's view, Douglass's revelation that his father was white connects him physically and literally to the white world. Niemtzow also believes that Douglass as a young boy embraced the white construction of himself as an animal and tried to shed his African skin. The scene to which Niemtzow is referring is the occasion when Douglass was encouraged to remove all the dead skin from his feet and knees before he left Colonel Lloyd's plantation for a "cleaner" Baltimore milieu. Niemtzow reads Douglass's account as a symbolic shedding of his African self for a new and improved white self. She argues that in this way, Douglass not only rejects his familial ties but also disassociates himself from his first home.[37]

Niemtzow also maintains that Jacobs's notion of womanhood is defined by the limitations that white culture imposed upon the literary genre of the female domestic novel. She insists that Jacobs fashions a text that falls short of autobiographical form as it mirrors the domestic novel's articulations of female chastity and marital compliance. Niemtzow suggests that Jacobs's decision to adhere to the structures of the domestic novel ultimately render her silent on the sexual transgressions committed against her. Jacobs is denied the freedom to explicitly express that she was raped and the reader is left with a sugarcoated account of an insolent "seduction."[38]

Niemtzow underestimated the extent to which Douglass and Jacobs embraced African culture. Indeed, they both appreciated and cherished the African values of their grandmothers. Referring to the respect between younger and older slaves on the Lloyd plantation, Douglass expressed that "there is no better material in the world for making a gentleman than is furnished in the African."[39] Jacobs believed that the greatest attraction of the Christmas season was the annual African-inspired John Kunering parade and she, like Douglass, offered illuminating commentary on slave dance, conjuration, and divination.[40]

In 1987 the discussion of the slave narrative returned, albeit briefly, to the annals of the historian. This was the year that Sterling Stuckey's *Slave Culture* and Peter Kolchin's *Unfree Labor* appeared. Stuckey's work made use of the narratives of Frederick Douglass and to a lesser extent those of William Wells Brown and Sojourner Truth to support his claim that African ethnicity was the principal means of black solidarity in the slavery era.[41] Kolchin's comparative study on Russian serfdom and American slavery, on the other hand, charges that the slave narratives are first and foremost memoirs of cultural disruption infused with Anglo religious sentiments. He reasons that Russian serfs were able to find greater success at achieving cultural autonomy than their slave counterparts due to the pervasive nature of planter paternalism that existed throughout American slave milieus. Africans, unlike Russian peasants in his view, underwent a cultural emasculation and became quite ashamed of conjuration and other not unrelated folk practices.[42]

Stuckey emerged as the greater authority on slave life with his unparalleled familiarity with a wide range of sources ranging from folktales, songs, and narratives to anthropological studies and ethnographic reports.

Stuckey revisited the narratives of Frederick Douglass at length in his essay "'Ironic Tenacity': Frederick Douglass's Seizure of the Dialectic" published in Eric Sundquist's edited book *Frederick Douglass: New Literary and Historical Essays* (1990). This essay broke ground in narrative studies as Stuckey was the first to extensively consider the ways in which African values found their way into a slave narrative. He explains that Douglass captured the African elements of joy and sorrow that were so much a part of the slave spirituals. Stuckey also reveals the careful attention that Douglass gave to African labor patterns. Prior to his investigation, except for a few exceptions, the consensus among scholars was that slave narratives had little to tells us of African culture within the slave quarters.[43]

Scholars have continued to view slave narratives as texts of cultural discontinuity. Sterling Bland, Jr.'s *Voices of the Fugitives* (2000) is one such analysis. Like most critics, Bland examines the white political, social, religious, and artistic forms that shaped the narratives but fails to provide an assessment of African influences. It is his contention that ex-slaves were unable to maneuver through the strict cultural boundaries imposed on the genre by white abolitionists and their white audiences, leaving the authors of slave narratives little option but to internalize white notions of their own identities.[44] He argues from the traditional assumption that black political and religious ideologies were traceable to the abolitionists' democratic principles of the Enlightenment and that white Christian theology served as the only stimulus for black ideas of freedom and equality. While Bland argues that Frederick Douglass, for example, was unable to rhetorically define and control his own environment he seems to contradict himself by explaining that Douglass had a cultural connection to Africa through the conjure doctor Sandy Jenkins. Yet he does not explore the Africanity of Douglass or any other black abolitionist in any depth. In fact, Bland postulates that Douglass's connection to Sandy is one of the few instances that Douglass situates his personal history in the context of African-American encouragement and support.[45]

Patrick Rael crafts similar interpretations to those put forth by Bland in his *Black Identity & Black Protest in the Antebellum North* (2002). While primarily concerned with oratorical public expressions of black dissent, Rael's locates the genesis of the moral ideology found in both the speeches and writings of blacks in "Anglo American thought."[46] He cautions against a cultural reading of African continuities through public mediums because the "rhetorical exigencies of operating within public sphere discourse often circumvented the operations of *culture.*" Since whites viewed black folk culture as inferior, Rael argues, there was little if any room for African or African-American influences. Suggesting that black folk culture was devoid of the mechanics for public debate, he concludes that black leaders only found appreciation for white culture and insists that favorable invocations of Africa are weak indicators for cultural continuities and identity formation. References to Africa by newly freed blacks, in Rael's view, had much more to do with their desire to be recognized as people with an authentic national heritage worthy of parity in public affairs than with an actual familiarity with African culture.[47] Another example of this view comes from Sylvia Frey, who argues that Africa did not have a revolutionary tradition and that the evangelicalism of republican ideology "formed the intellectual foundation for the incipient antislavery movements in England and in the northern colonies."[48]

The historiographical tradition of the slave narrative is not unrelated to the scholarship on U.S. abolitionism. Both have generally silenced the African cultural role of blacks and in most studies concerning the former the ex-slave is absent altogether. To be certain, Benjamin Quarles and Jane and William H. Pease have written rather extensive tracts on the subject of black abolitionism and Herbert Aptheker, Merton L. Dillon, Paul Goodman and a few others have broached it. Their accounts, however, have been limited to a national analysis that does not extend beyond U.S. borders.[49]

When both the genre of the slave narrative and the theme of American abolitionism are probed, scholars shy away from considering the revolutionary and cultural tradition found in both discourses, which often overlap, in light of the African historical background. It as if the spirit of reform and morality infused with economic and labor concerns—the very tone in which the popular book length narratives of the Garrisonian period addressed their readers—only enjoyed antecedents in Euro-American thought. It was through these very currents that some historians and literary critics argue that the idea of slavery as a sinful social evil emerges. And while scholars continue to debate the degree of influence that moral and economic factors had on both the early more moderate gradualist anti-slavery movement and the post 1830's radicals who called for the immediate abolishment of slavery, most agree that the moral-religious mood during the second half of the eighteenth century was primarily inspired by Euro-American thought. Convinced that the second Great Awakening led by Charles G. Finney encouraged the younger generation to reject the sin of slavery, Gilbert H. Barnes during the 1930s for example, was among the first to locate abolitionism within the context of the evangelist movement.[50]

John McKivigan's edited volume; *History of the American Abolitionist Movement* (1999) is an example of related scholarship. McKivigan asserts that the selected essays for the series marks a shift in the historiography away from linking the birth of abolitionism to class tensions or psychological disorders towards associating the movement's beginnings with the Enlightenment and the propensity of evangelical Christians to associate slavery with sin. McKivigan's text is on course with most of what has been written on the origins of American abolitionism.[51] Providing an uneven portrait of the early Atlantic world by neglecting to consider African cultural influences, these treatments have in many ways paralleled analyses of the slave narrative and the related black antebellum protest movements. Black abolitionist ideology did not mysteriously spring up out of thin air, nor was it solely the result of Anglo influences. An adequate assessment of black anti-slavery sentiment must take into account African attempts to abolish the trade in slaves and also evaluate the ways in which such efforts were linked to resistance movements in the early U.S. and black abolitionist efforts of the nineteenth century.

While Sierra Leone, the Gold Coast, the Bight of Benin, the Bight of Biafra, West Central Africa and Mozambique-Madagascar all held cultural and political significance for the New World, Senegambia, because of its relative propinquity to Europe, was among the first to participate in the Atlantic trading complex with sizable exports of slaves reaching the shores of early North America. Hence, it is in large part to Senegambia, a region responsible for igniting a succession of uprisings in the surrounding polities, that expatriates owed the development of the nascent slave community and its proclivity towards a non-secular revolutionary tradition.[52] In view of the foregoing, a look at Senegambia during the era of the overseas slave trade will help to better locate the revolutionary tradition that emerged on the other side of the Atlantic.

Comprising the stretch of land on the upper Guinea coast that encircles the Senegal and Gambia rivers, Senegambia is delineated by Futu Toro in the North and Futa Jallon in the south. The Portuguese established trading networks in the region as early as the fifteenth century. Its hegemony, however, became challenged by the hasty construction of Dutch, French, and British trading factories during the seventeenth century. It was only a matter of time before Senegambia's economy became burdened by the shift in gold, ivory, wax, cereal, leather, and slave trade away from trans-Saharan routes towards Atlantic arteries for New World markets. The swing in the direction of these trade goods, especially slaves, undermined the socio-economic stability of the region as the labor source increasingly dwindled. A number of confederacies, including the Berber-Jolof union in the north, became severely weakened. This intensified the already strained political relationship between the Hasaniyya Arab military rulers (*ceedo*), who were trekking southward in hopes of profiting from Atlantic trade and the Sanhadja marabouts of present day Mauritania who were concerned with maintaining trans-Saharan trade networks.

Marabout interests were defended for a brief time by the Moor Nasir al-Din. Igniting a religious-political movement in 1673 against contemporary military aristocracies who supported the overseas slave trade, Nasir al-Din, in his role as a clerical leader, sought not only to solve the economic problems that the northern river valley states of Wallo, Futa Toro, Kayor, and Jolof were facing, but also decided to revamp Islam by proclaiming that the overseas slave trade was inhumane and thereby contrary to the tenets of the faith. [53] According to Michael Gomez, Nasir al-Din was able to marshal support of the Wolof peasantry by condemning the participation of the elite in the slave trade, insisting that "God does not allow kings to plunder, kill or make their people captive."[54] Gomez also points out that Nasir al-Din recruited a number of followers by claiming that an imminent supernatural harvest would assure their sustenance so that there was no need for agricultural endeavors.[55]

Nasir al-Din's marabout movement enjoyed some success throughout the Senegal Valley—a stronghold of the French. Under his direction, Islam increasingly expanded beyond traders and merchants as the ceedo military elite was replaced with new clerical leadership known as "chief prayer leaders."[56] For those unable to enjoy the profits of slavery, religion was becoming a viable vehicle for resistance, albeit the initial victories of the marabout insurgents were short-lived.

The movement was unable to cope with the murder of its prophetic clerical leader Nasir al-Din who was killed by Hassaniyya forces in 1674 whom the French supported. From the French perspective, nothing was to be gained from a potential unified Islamic front capable of dictating the course of the slave trade. Consequently, they supported the restoration of the old ceedo aristocratic regimes, most of which were reinstated by 1677.

The movement was also weakened when Nasir al Din's men broke their promise and began to participate in the overseas trading system. Yet, this did not break the revolutionary spirit of those opposed to the slave trade, and though opposition forces thwarted the marabout movement, it was not obliterated. In fact, a number of marabout families continued to forge close ties along puritanical Islamic lines advocating the end of ceedo rule and the Trans-Atlantic slave trade. Many of the insurgents, however, were forced to convene clandestinely in order to avoid the constant attacks against Muslims.

The hostile living situation eventually led to great numbers of marabouts abandoning coastal areas for the safer Bundu and Futa Jallon regions. It was in these polities that the movement resurfaced. In Bundu, Gomez tells us that Maalik Sy established a Muslim state on behalf of the Jakhanke marabouts around 1690 in which he, like Nasir-al Din, functioned as an Islamic religious leader. Maalik Sy learned from Nasir al-Din's mistakes and recognized the need for establishing a pragmatic state that was tolerant of religious and ethnic differences. Similar Muslim revolutions also occurred in Futa Jallon and Futa Toro during the early eighteenth century and 1760s respectively. Signaling the rising Islamic militancy, these latter movements were a response to the increasing rigidity of the slave trade.[57]

While there is no direct evidence at this time linking the U.S. anti-slavery movements to the Senegambian marabout movement, it seems probable that the slaves' critique of the U.S. religious slavocracy and along with their incorporation of African political and cultural forms that we find throughout the slave narratives are in some ways linked to Senegambian resistance and religious pragmatism. Certainly Senegambia was not the only region that resisted the slave trade nor was it the only polity capable of bequeathing its political ideology to those who journeyed across the Atlantic.[58] However, it is likely that Senegambia was one of and perhaps the first contributor to the political principles and cultural ethos accepted by antebellum blacks. In his study of political and cultural pragmatism in the Senegambian refugee state of eighteenth-century Bundu, Michael Gomez reveals that in an effort to secure the state's stability the religious toleration of the day allowed for the incorporation of multiple beliefs. The historical context of the trans-Atlantic slave trade along with the wide range of ethnic groups from which slaves were drawn provided for a related pragmatism throughout American slave communities. Before proceeding a succinct discussion of importation rates from the region is needed.

Estimates suggest that Senegambia was responsible for 14.5% (64,636) of the total African imports into British North America with most transported before the middle of the eighteenth century. Though numbers declined after 1750, Britain still exported slightly more than 10,000 Senegambians during the 1770s.[59] Only a small percentage of this total probably made it to the mainland colonies. Nonetheless, it is likely that those coming from the areas surrounding Futa Toro would have served as a reminder of the intense battles for power and autonomy to both native-born and second-generation Senegambians—many of whom would have been familiar with the political gains and losses resulting from the string of Muslim revolutions aimed at challenging the power structure of the trans-Atlantic slave trade dating back to the late seventeenth century.[60]

Pre-eighteenth-century written records of blacks petitioning against American slavery and the slave trade are few and far between. Herbert Aptheker, however, has documented roughly two hundred and fifty acts of southern and northern conspiracies and revolts throughout the slave era in which the very actions of the mutineers and or conspirators reflected their inherent anti-slavery aspirations. This unrelenting mood of insurgency triggered stricter slave laws in a number of states. Aptheker points out that New York, for example, as a result of a 1712 conspiracy ratified a "law 'for preventing, Suppressing and punishing the Conspiracy and Insurrection of Negroes and other Slaves.' The same event was also important in leading to a measure adopted by Massachusetts in 1713 forbidding further importation of slaves, and a Pennsylvania act of August, 1712, placing a high duty on Negroes, thus effectually discouraging their importation."[61] Since Senegambians residing in the rice growing regions of the slave south tended to abscond, any number of them may have ended up in the North where a strong black anti-slavery tradition existed.[62] Furthermore, Senegambians are mentioned in runaway notices coming out of Louisiana and others from the state were implicated in a 1731 plot driven by abolitionist ideas.[63]

Regarded as the founding father of black masonry in America, Prince Hall was among the first blacks to craft formal petitions advocating the end of slavery and the trade in slaves during the 1770s. There is no firm evidence that Hall or his work had a direct relationship with the genre of nineteenth-century slave narratives or the revolutionary tradition of Senegambians in the New World. Yet, the timing of his petitions not only coincides with the American Revolution, as his biographers have noted, but it also overlaps with the Futa Toro Islamic Revolution in Senegambia.[64] Furthermore, petitions against slavery and the slave trade on this side of the Atlantic share the same fundamental denunciation of the immoral and unjust power structure that was pervasive among many eighteenth-century Senegambians and a number of slave narrators, including Frederick Douglass, William Wells Brown, Harriet Tubman, and Harriet Jacobs gravitated towards a similar critique of American slavery.

In a 1777 petition presented to the Massachusetts House of Representatives, Hall declared that a

> Great Number of Blackes detained in a State of slavery in the Bowels of a free & Christian Country Humbly shuwith that your Petitioners apprehend that they have in Common with all other men a Natural and Unaliable Right to that freedom which the Grat Parent of the Unavers hath Bestowed equalley on all menkind and which they have Never forfuted by any Compact or agreement whatever-but they wher Unjustly Dragged by the hand of cruel Power from their Derest friends and sum of them Even torn from the Embraces of their tender

Parents-from A populous Pleasant and plentiful contry and in viola-
tion of Laws of Nature and off Nations and in defiance of all the tender feelings of humanity Brough hear Either to Be sold Like Beast of
Burthen & Like them Condemnd to Slavery for Life-Among A People
Profesing the mild Religion of Jesus A people Not Insensible of the
Secrets of Rationable Being Nor without spirit to Resent the unjust
endeavours of others to Reduce them to a state of Bondage and Sub-
jection your honouer Need not to be informed that A Life of Slavery
Like that of your petioners Deprived of Every social privilege of Every
thing Requiset to Render Life Tolable is far worse then Nonexistence.
In imitation of the Lawdable Example of the Good People of these
States your petiononers have Long and Patiently waited the Evnt of
petition after petition By them presented to the Legislative Body of
this state and cannot but with Grief Reflect that their Sucess hath teen
but too similar they Cannot but express their Astonishment that It
has Never Bin Consirdered that Every Principle from which Amarica
has Acted in the Cours of their unhappy Deficultes vvith Great Briton
Pleads Stronger than A thousand arguments in favowrs of your petioners they therfor humble Beseech your honours to give this peti[ti]
on its due weight & consideration and cause an act of the Legislatur
to be past Wherby they may Be Restored to the Enjoyments of that
which is the Naturel Right of all men and their Children who wher
Born in this Land of Liberty may not be heald as Slaves after they
arive at the age of Twenty-one years so may the Inhabitance of thes
Stats No longer chargeable with the inconsistancey of acting themselves the part which they condem and oppose in others Be prospered
in their present Glorious struggle for Liberty and have those Blessing
to them, &c.[65]

While Hall's challenge to the religious and ethical morality of the slave
power may have drawn on the rhetorical strategies of the enlightenment, his
formative years in the active port city of Bridgetown, located in the sugar
colony of Barbados would have not been without influence. Hall did not
arrive to Boston until the age of seventeen in 1765 on a British trading vessel. He would have likely recalled the anti-slavery agitation of both slaves
and free blacks in Barbados. It is also quite probable that he would have
witnessed the infamous Bridgetown *cages* that Hillary Beckles describes in
her investigation of female slave resistance in the colony. Serving as holding
cells for recalcitrant slaves who ran away, fugitives would remain incarcerated here in deplorable conditions until their owners reclaimed them. The
Gold Coast supplied the largest number of slaves to Barbados. Yet it is
not beyond reason to conclude that Senegambians were among the island's
dissenters. This may have been especially true during the 1710s through
the 1730s when British slave imports from Senegambia soared. Moreover,
up until the mid-eighteenth-century Britain acquired one sixth of its total

imports from Senegambia, many of whom would have been transported to Barbados. In effect then, Barbadian culture and politics was not without Senegambian influence where a similar religious and moral critique against the slaveocracy was already in place.

These eighteenth-century antislavery expressions are in many ways a subgenre of the early slave narrative and offer a rather unique voice of antebellum blacks. Unlike the authors of slave narratives they were not constrained by the publisher's agenda. While there may not have been a pervasive class consciousness or revolutionary spirit in the written slave narrative prior to the height of the abolitionist movement in the 1830s, such a consciousness, though varying in form and structure, did exist in the larger folk narrative of colonial blacks through the petition movement. Finding a more unfavorable representation of the slaveholder during the latter period, Marion Starling as we have mentioned, argues that the slave narratives preceding the 1830s tended to minimize class consciousness while those of the abolitionist period did not.[66] Similarly, Willaim Andrews argues that the early narratives reflect a powerless slave community that was constantly subjected to white cultural values.[67] Echoing Andrews, Valerie Smith writes from the paternalist assumption that the early narrative presents blacks one dimensionally—culturally assimilated and ever desiring protections that only whites could provide.[68] Yet, as shown above, when the more radical sentiment of immediatist abolitionism does appear in the nineteenth-century narrative, not only did it already enjoy a tradition in the seventeenth-century petition movement but it was also rooted in African ant-islavery movements. One need not go any further than the slave narratives to observe the ways blacks fashioned their beliefs on the religion and morality of the ruling class—beliefs which also recall the eighteenth-century petition movement.

Notes

NOTES TO THE PREFACE

1. John Morley, Introduction to *The Complete Poetical Works of William Wordsworth* (New York: Thomas Y. Crowell Company Publishers, 1907), 209. [Italics mine].
2. Arna Bontemps, *Black Thunder* (Macmillian Company, 1936; repr.; Boston: Beacon Press, 1992), 157–193.
3. Hunter Davies, *William Wordsworth: A Biography* (New York: Atheneum, 1980), 48, 52.
4. Bontemps, xvi-xix.
5. Ibid., xxvi.
6. Ibid., xix.
7. Ibid., 165–167.
8. Ibid., 166.
9. See Arna Bontemps, *Great Slave Narratives* (Boston: Beacon Press, 1969).
10. Bontemps, *Black Thunder*, 163.
11. Marion W. Starling, *The Slave Narrative: Its Place in American History* (Washington, D.C.: Howard University Press, 1988), xxvi, 311.
12. See Peter Kolchin, *Unfree Labor: American Slavery and Russian Serfdom* (Cambridge: Belknap, 1987), 227–228; Annetee Niemtzow, "The Problematic Self in Autobiography," in John Sekora and Darwin Turner, eds., *The Art of Slave Narrative: Original Essays in Criticism and Theory* (Western Illinois: University Press, 1982), 8, 19. Sterling Bland Jr., *Voices of the Fugitives: Runaway Slave Stories and their Stories of Self-Creation* (Connecticut: Praeger, 2000), 25–26.

NOTES TO CHAPTER 1

1. Waldo Martin Jr., *The Mind of Frederick Douglass* (Chapel Hill and London: UNC Press, 1984), 4, 5, 22, 200; Dickson J. Preston, *Young Frederick Douglass* (London: John Hopkins, 1980), 10.
2. Stanley Harold, *American Abolitionists* (New York: Longman, 2001), 25, 65–66.
3. Waldo Martin Jr. labeled Douglass as an integrationist and an assimilationist. See Martin, 219.
4. Sterling Stuckey argues that Douglass was not far removed from African culture, but scholars have not expanded upon Stuckey's valuable contribution. Sterling Stuckey, "'Ironic Tenacity': Frederick Douglass's Seizure of the

Dialectic," in Eric Sundquist's, ed., *Frederick Douglass: New Literary and Historical Essays* (Cambridge: University Press, 1990), 23–41.

5. Benjamin Quarles, *Frederick Douglass* (Washington: Associated Publishers, 1948); Phillip Foner, *Frederick Douglass, A Biography* (New York: Citadel, 1964), 369–370. Martin, 20, 254, 169. When William McFeely provided his treatment of Douglass in 1991, he made a compelling argument that Douglass may have been a descendant of Senegambian Muslims from Futa Jalon. Nonetheless he did not stray too far from the traditional view that Douglass's primary influences were Christianity and white culture. William McFeely, *Frederick Douglass* (New York: Norton, 1991), 5. Dickson J. Preston argued that Douglass's and other blacks in Talbot County were far removed from African culture. Preston, 10.

6. Due to the limited source material on African culture predating the twentieth century and the limited synchronic approach of colonial anthropologies on Africa, historians are presented with the formidable task of working with such records, thereby making the process of discerning which cultural patterns originated from what region and among which class an arduous one. Hence, the inferential is often hard to avoid. Nevertheless, Michael Gomez, Sterling Stuckey, Margaret Washington, Creel Washington and others have made rather strong cases for the existence of specific and direct cultural links between Africa and the mainland colonies. My intention here, then, is not to reinvent the wheel but rather show through a comparative textual analysis how ex-slave narratives served as a collective memory of Africans on this side of the Atlantic by pointing to corresponding cultural examples.

7. Frederick Douglass, "My Bondage and My Freedom" (1855; repr.; in *Douglass Autobiographies*, New York: Penguin, 1994), 142. Despite only having a short-lived relationship with his mother, Harriet Bailey, Douglass recognized her ancestral presence after she passed away. He learned after her death that she was the only colored person in Tuckahoe who enjoyed the privilege of literacy. "In view of this fact," he writes "I am happy to attribute any love of letters I may have, not to my presumed Anglo-Saxon paternity, but to the native genius of my sable, unprotected, and uncultivated mother—a woman who belonged to a race whose mental endowments are still disparaged and despised." It is likely that Douglass' deep appreciation for his mother's ability to read had much to do with him calling her to mind during an 1836 plot to escape from slavery. It was then that he became imbued with an uncanny feeling that the plan had been exposed. In addition to sharing his impressions with one of his co-conspirators, Sandy Jenkins, Douglass subtly affirmed a connection to his mother. He writes, "If my mother—then long in her grave—had appeared before me, and told me that we were betrayed, I could not, at that moment, have felt more certain of the fact." *My Bondage*, 316.

8. Her nets were in high demand in Denton, Tuckahoe and Hillsboro. Douglass, *My Bondage*, 141.

9. Ibid.

10. See Mike Gomez, *Exchanging Our Country Marks* (Chapel Hill and London: University of North Carolina Press, 1998) 124–125.

11. Percy Amaury Talbot, *Life in Southern Nigeria* (London: Oxford University Press, 1926), 223. Charles Kingsley Meek provides further insight on Nigerian yam festivals. See Meek, *Law and Authority in a Nigerian Tribe* (London: Oxford University Press, 1937), 26.

12. A.B. Ellis, *The Tshi-Speaking Peoples of the Slave Coast of West Africa* (London: Chapman & Hall, Ltd., 1887), 229.

13. Douglass, *My Bondage*, 143, 148.

14. Scott C. Williamson in his recent study on Douglass does not take into account the Africans Douglass encountered on the Lloyd plantation. "That he was raised within a community of Americanized slaves," he asserts, "several generations removed from Africa, and with an extended history on the Eastern Shore, are important to his early self-understanding and rapport with his master's family." Scott C. Williamson, *The Moral and Religious Thought of Frederick Douglass: The Narrative Life* (Georgia: Mercer University, 2002), 2.
15. Douglass, *My Bondage*, 149
16. Frederick Douglass, "Life and Times of Frederick Douglass" (1893; repr.; *Douglass Autobiographies*, New York: Penguin, 1994), 486. Such crafts would not have been unfamiliar to Africans. See Juliet E. Walker, *The History of Black Business in America* (New York: Macmillian Library Ref), 1998, 1–31. P. Diagne, "African Political, Economic and Social Structures During this period" in B.A. Ogot, eds., *Africa from the Sixteenth to the Eighteenth Century* (London: Heinemann; Berkley, University of California Press, Paris: UNESCO, 1992), 26–34. As was typically the case, their rations of food and garments were meager and punishments were handed out in abundance. See also Douglass, "Narrative of the Life of Frederick Douglass, An American Slave" (1845; repr., *Douglass Autobiographies*, New York: Penguin, 1994). 22; Douglass, *My Bondage*, 401.
17. Gomez, *Exchanging Our Country Marks*, 47.
18. Douglass, *Life and Times*, 490.
19. Ibid.
20. Douglass, *My Bondage*, 164–165. Though his prescriptions drew mainly on western medicinal items he still functioned as a conjure doctor by seeking to heal his patients both spiritually and physically.
21. Scholars who assert that the solidarity among slaves was undermined by their unyielding attachment to their paternalistic kind-loving Christian masters have paid little attention to Douglass's observations. "Uncle" as was "Aunt" were used as a terms of endearment and respect. Douglass quickly dismissed the stereotypical notion that slaves did not get along. "I never loved any or confided in any people more than my fellow-slaves." In fact, for Douglass slavery was anything but benign or patriarchal. Slaves could not afford to forsake each other for the "protections" that only masters could provide. "If kindness were the rule, we should not see advertisements filling the columns of almost every southern newspaper, offering large rewards for fugitive slaves, and describing them as being branded with irons, loaded with chains, and scarred by the whip." He later added, "the slave finds more of the milk of human kindness in the bosom of the savage Indian, than in the heart of his *Christian master.*" For the aforementioned passages see respectively, *My Bondage*,35, 153, 426; *Narrative*, 78; *My Bondage*.
22. Douglass, *My Bondage*, 141.
23. Ibid., 160.
24. Frederick Douglass, *Narrative*, 24–26. Douglass expanded upon the antislavery sentiment of these songs in *My Bondage*: "It would seem almost absurd to say it, considering the use that has been made of them, that we have allies in the Ethiopian songs; those songs that constitute our national music, and without which we have no national music. They are heart songs, and the finest feelings of human nature are expressed in them . . . [they] can make the heart sad as well as merry, and can call forth a tear as well as a smile. They awaken the sympathies for the slave, in which anti-slavery principles take root, grow, and flourish." See *My Bondage*, 449–450. These same songs probably inspired Douglass to sing whenever he was "pretty severely pinched

by hunger." His songs served as pleas for food to Miss Lurcretia who must have been quite pleased with his musical efforts as she often rewarded him. See *My Bondage*, 207.

25. For a fuller discussion of the ring shout see Harold Courlander, *Negro Folk Music, U.S.A.* (New York: Columbia University Press, 1963; reprint, New York: Dover Publications, 1991), 194–200; Sterling Stuckey, *Slave Culture: Nationalist Theory & the Foundations of Black America* (New York and Oxford: Oxford University Press, 1988), 12.

26. As late as the 1870s Payne, like most black elite and high ranking clergymen, was unsuccessful in his attempts to rid the ring shout ceremony at various A.M.E. churches in the District of Columbia, Pennsylvania, Maryland and other northern places that he had visited. Daniel Payne, *Recollections of Seventy Years* (1888; repr., New York: Arno Press, 1968), 254–256.

27. Douglass, *My Bondage*, 188. [Italics mine]. Here one is reminded of Thomas Wentworth Higginson's observations of the shout in the Sea Islands during the Civil War: "All over the camp the lights glimmer in the tents, and as I sit at my desk in the open doorway, there come mingled sounds of stir and glee. Boys laugh and shout—a feeble flute stirs somewhere in some tent, not an officer's—drums throb not far away in another." This "laugh" is likely a result of the "frenzy" in which the body is mounted by one's ancestors and or other deities. See Thomas W. Higginson, *Army Life in a Black Regiment* (Boston: Lee and Shepard, 1890), 41.

28. Douglass, *Life and Times*, 1013. It is erroneous to conclude that because one was an integrationist, they were consequently detached from African culture. However, this was not an uncommon viewpoint during the nineteenth century.

29. Lucy Chase to her family, March 4, in Henry L. Swint, ed., *Dear Ones at Home: Letters from Contraband Camps* (Nashville, 1966), 58. [Italics Mine]. Douglass's remarks also call to mind Sterling Stuckey's analysis of Herman Melville's treatment of Ashantee dance in *Benito Cereno*. In the novel, it was the six Ashantees who danced like "delirious black *dervishes*" in a counter-clockwise fashion. Stuckey found that Melville's reference to "black dervishes" was probably informed by T. E. Bowdich's discussion of Ashantee circular dance. See T. E. Bowdich, *Mission to Cape Coast Castle and Ashantee* (1819; reprint third ed., London: Frank Cass & Co., 1966), p. 40; Sterling Stuckey, "The Tambourine in Glory" in Robert S. Levine, eds., *The Cambridge Companion to Herman Melville* (New York: Cambridge University Press, 1998), 57, 63. Thomas Wentworth Higginson's writing on the ring shout echoes Melville and Douglass: "Some "heel and toe" tumultuously, others merely tremble and stagger on, others stoop and rise, others whirl, others caper sideways, all keep steadily circling like *dervishes*." [Italics mine.] See Higginson, 41. Fredrika Bremer observed similar scenes at a Methodist class meeting in New Orleans during the 1850s. Bremer witnessed "a real African tornado" in which some of the exhorters "began to leap—leaped aloft with a motion as of a cork flying out of a bottle, while they waved their arms and their handkerchiefs in the air, as if they were endeavoring to bring something down, and all the while crying aloud, 'Come, oh come!' And as they leaped, they twisted their bodies round in a sort of corkscrew fashion, and were evidently in a state of convulsion; sometimes they fell down and rolled in the aisle, amid loud, lamenting cries and groans." Fredrika Bremer, *America of the Fifties: Letters of Fredrika*, ed. Adolph B. Benson (New York: Oxford U. Press, 1924), 274–276.

30. Douglass, *My Bondage*, 367. Yet, he would not waver in his stringent and intelligent denunciation of the peculiar institution and it was for this reason

that many of his northern listeners initially found his story dubious. "He is educated," they heralded "and is, in this, a contradiction of all the facts we have concerning the ignorance of slaves." It would prove to be this same prejudice that inspired Douglass to print his own weekly anti-slavery newspaper, *North Star*, in Rochester, New York in 1847. He was convinced that "the greatest hindrance to the adoption of abolition principles by the people of the United States was the low estimate everywhere in that country placed upon the negro as a man." It was Douglass's opinion that a black newspaper would help mitigate these cultural biases, and found an equally suitable platform to do so in his narratives.

31. Douglass, *Life and Times*, 492.
32. Ibid., 609. Then there was also the tendency for the slaves to adhere to the maxim "a still tongue makes a wise head," when asked about their treatment. Knowing that it was not uncommon to have planted moles in their company ready to betray their confidence it was to their advantage to speak favorably of their conditions.
33. Douglass, *My Bondage*, 168.
34. Frederick Douglass (1854), quoted in *The Frederick Douglass Papers*, ed. John W. Blassingame et al., 5 vols. (New York: Yale University Press, 1979) 2: 517.
35. Ibid.
36. Ibid., 519. Waldo Martin Jr. neglected to consider Douglass's comments on language when he argued that Douglass was repulsed by West African culture. Martin, 4–5, 22.
37. Douglass (1865), quoted in Blassingame, *The Frederick Douglass Papers*, 4: 165.
38. Douglass (1865), in Blassingame, *The Frederick Douglass Papers*, 4: 93–95.
39. Douglass (1854), in Blassingame, *The Frederick Douglass Papers*, 2: 519.
40. Douglass, *My Bondage*, 169.
41. Robert G. O'Meally, "The Vernacular Tradition" in Henry Louis Gates Jr., eds., *The Norton Anthology to African American Literature* (New York: W.W. Norton & Co., 1997), 1–4.
42. Lawrence Levine, *Black Culture and Black Consciousness* (New York: Oxford U Press, 1977), 147.
43. Douglass, *My Bondage*, 169.
44. Levine, 146; Lorenzo D. Turner, *Africanisms in the Gullah Dialect* (Chicago, 1949), 11–14; Turner, "Problems Confronting the Investigator of Gullah," *Publications of the American Dialect Society*, No. 9 (1947), 74–84.
45. Douglass, *My Bondage*, 169.
46. Douglass, *Life and Times*, 492.
47. Theophus H. Smith, *Conjuring Culture* (New York and Oxford: Oxford U Press, 1994).
48. Smith, 4–6.
49. Zora Neale Hurston, *Mules and Men* (New York: Harper and Row, 1990), 280; Harry Middleton Hyatt, *Hoodoo, Conjuration, Witchcraft, Rootwork*, Vol. 1 (Missouri: Western Publishing, 1970), 103. Similarly Lawrence Levine maintained that "conjurers could be pictured as exotic Old Testament type prophets or magicians." Levine *Black Culture and Black Consciousness*, 74.
50. Regarding this transfer as one of the significant turning points in his life he admitted that "I may be deemed superstitious, and even egotistical, in regarding this event as a special interposition of divine Providence in my favor. But I should be false to the earliest sentiments of my soul, if I suppressed the opinion." Douglass, *Narrative*, 36.

51. While laboring under the direction of Covey Douglass came to fully understand how his lot compared to that of an oxen. "They were property," he writes "so was I; they were to be broken, so was I." *My Bondage*, 263.

52. Douglass, *Narrative*, 60.

53. Douglass, *My Bondage*, 282.

54. Douglass, *My Bondage*, 281. C.K. Meek described similar beliefs held by Nigeria natives: "The believer in witchcraft feels he has a right to protect himself by every means in his power, and chief among these is the employment of a witch-doctor . . . [who] is therefore considered just as essential in most negro communities as a medical practitioner is amongst ourselves, and, though some witch-doctors may abuse their powers for selfish ends, as a class they are regarded as champions of morality." Meek, 345. Providing further insight on the matter Alan Menzies, writing of West African linguistic groups says: "There is generally a special person . . . who knows these things, and is able to work them. He has more power over spirits than other men have, and is able to make them do what he likes. He can heal sickness, he can foretell the future, he can change a thing into something else, or a man into a lower animal, or a tree, or anything; he can also assume such transformations himself at will. He uses means to bring about such results; he knows about herbs, he has also recourse to rubbing, to making images of affected parts in the body, and to various other arts . . . It is the spirit dwelling in him which brings about the wonderful results; without the sprit he could not do anything." Menzies, *History of Religion: A Sketch of Primitive Religious Beliefs and Practices and of the Origin and Character of the Great Systems* (New York: Scribner's Sons, 1897), 73.

55. Douglass, *Narrative*, 70. Writing on the Yoruba A. B. Ellis remarked: "They consequently attribute sickness and death, other than death resulting from injury or violence, to persons who have for bad purposes enlisted the services of evil spirits, that is to say, to wizards and witches." Ellis, *The Yoruba-Speaking Peoples of the Slave Coast of West Africa* (London: Chapman & Hall, Ltd., 1894), 117. C. K. Meek explained that among the Jukun "Sudden deaths, especially of young people, are usually regarded as the work of sorcerers (*ba-shiko or ba-shibu*). If the deceased had been noted for his disrespect to his seniors his death would be ascribe to offended ancestors, and he would go to his grave with 'blood-shot eyes'; but otherwise it is thought that one who had died suddenly had met his death by the foul means of witchcraft and would take vengeance in his own time." Meek, *A Sudanese Kingdom and Ethnographical Study of the Jukun-Speaking Peoples of Nigeria* (London: Kegan, 1931), 223–24. Writing on the Mpongwe Robert Milligan says: "Sickness and death, they believe, may be caused by fetish medicine, which need not be administered to the victim, but is usually laid beside the path where he is about to pass." Milligan, *The Fetish Folk of West Africa* (New York: Fleming H. Revell Co., 1912), 39. Robert Hamill Nassau claimed "according to native ideas, all over Africa, such a thing as death from natural causes does not exist. Whatever ill befalls a man or family, it is always the result of witchcraft, and in every case the witch-doctors are consulted to find out who has been guilty of it." Nassau, *Fetichism in West Africa*. (New York: Charles Scribner's Sons, 1904), 117. Amaury Talbot says of the Ibibio of Nigeria: "When a man falls sick because his soul has gone forth and is being detained by an enemy, or when he believes that such as one is trying to entice it from out his body, he, in turn, goes to a Juju man known to have the power of seeing clearly." Talbot, *Life in Southern Nigeria* (London: Macmillan & Co., Ltd., 1923), 803. Early on in *Narrative of the Life of Frederick Douglass*, his first narrative, he makes no apologies

for what he terms the "superstitious" beliefs that were so much a part of his history in Talbot County. When Douglass received the news that he would be moving form the Lloyd plantation to the residence of Hugh and Sophia Auld in Baltimore in March of 1826 he regarded this transfer as one of the significant turning points in his life. "I may be deemed superstitious, and even egotistical, in regarding this event as a special interposition of divine Providence in my favor. But I should be false to the earliest sentiments of my soul, if I suppressed the opinion. I prefer to be true to myself, even at the hazard of incurring the ridicule of others, rather than to be false, and incur my own abhorrence. Douglass, *Narrative*, 36.

56. Douglass, *My Bondage*, 286, 309.

57. Ibid., 312–315. The Gold Coast which comprises contemporary Ghana contributed the second largest of slave imports to Maryland. Robert Rattray wrote of a similar belief concerning birds held by the Ashanti of Ghana: "A cock crowing at midnight or long before dawn is immediately killed, as it is considered unlucky." Rattray, *Ashanti Proverbs* (Oxford: The Clarendon Press, 1930), 80. Emma Monroe, a former slave of Tin City, Georgia located east of Savannah, described to interviewers what a howling owl meant to her: "A screech owl screechin roun tells yuh somebody neah by gwine die." Georgia Writer's Project, *Drums and Shadows* (Georgia: The University of Georgia Press, 1940), 18. The same interviewers learned from George Smith of Sapelo Island Georgia that "if an owl hoots on top of the house or near the house, it is supposed to be a sign of death." Ibid., 171. Author Arna Bontemps also captured the symbolic meaning of birds and their association with misfortune in his novel *Black Thunder*. Bontemps, *Black Thunder* (1936), repr., (Boston: Beacon, 1968).

58. Douglass, *My Bondage*, 313, 320. Dreams were not taken lightly by some of the descendants of the Georgia coastal slaves. Katie McCarts of Old Fort explained "dreams, I sho do believe in em. Jis fo my son wuz drowned I suttnly have a dream that mean a death in the fambly." There were others from White Bluff, Pinpoint, and Grimball's Point who also admitted a belief in the prophetic power of dreams. *Drums and Shadows*, 5, 77, 83, 99.

59. Douglass, *My Bondage*, 321. Writing on Douglass's relationship with Sandy, Waldo Martin argued that "Christianity—a symbol of Western culture—had prevailed over magic—a symbol of African culture. This fateful adolescent impression of Africa as a land of irreligion or superstition would also inform his adult impression of Africa and Africans." see Martin, *The Mind of Frederick Douglass*, 203.

60. Douglass (1849), quoted in Blassingame, *The Frederick Douglass Papers*, 2: 175.

61. Douglass, *Life and Times of Frederick Douglass* (1893; repr.; *Douglass Autobiographies*, New York: Penguin, 1994), 842. [italics mine]. C.K. Meek described similar beliefs held by Nigeria natives: "The believer in witchcraft feels he has a right to protect himself by every means in his power, and chief among these is the employment of a witch-doctor . . . [who] is therefore considered just as essential in most negro communities as a medical practitioner is amongst ourselves, and, though some witch-doctors may abuse their powers for selfish ends, as a class they are regarded as champions of morality." Meek, *Law and Authority in a Nigerian*, 345. Providing further insight on the matter Alan Menzies, writing of West African linguistic groups says: "There is generally a special person . . . who knows these things, and is able to work them. He has more power over spirits than other men have, and is able to make them do what he likes. He can heal sickness, he can foretell the future, he can change a thing into

something else, or a man into a lower animal, or a tree, or anything; he can also assume such transformations himself at will. He uses means to bring about such results; he knows about herbs, he has also recourse to rubbing, to making images of affected parts in the body, and to various other arts . . . It is the spirit dwelling in him which brings about the wonderful results; without the sprit he could not do anything." Menzies, 73.

62. Douglass, *My Bondage*, 231.
63. While on his spiritual pursuit he met Charles Lawson, a free black drayman, who had a distinctive religious character which impressed the young Douglass. The two developed a close relationship and *Uncle Lawson*, as he was called, became Douglass's "spiritual father." Again, "Uncle" here reinforces the fictive kinship associations that were vital to the slaves' sense of extended familial ties. Douglass and Lawson's secret meetings of ritualistic singing and praying went on for some time. Not quite able to read as well as Douglass, the mentor taught the pupil the "spirit" and in turn received lessons that increased his knowledge of "the letter." Ibid., 231–232. Around this time Douglass also read the *Columbian Orator*, an anthology of patriotic speeches imbued with the republican ideas of freedom and equality. The volume, edited by Caleb Bingham, was widely used to instruct schoolchildren on how to express themselves *properly*. Douglass was drawn to a number of the speeches and anecdotes included in the text which helped him to formulate a strong conviction in him that his race, contrary to the doctrine of most religious slaveholders, was not innately bound to servitude. Ibid., 226–227. Douglass first learned to read while staying with ship carpenter Hugh Auld and his wife Sophia in 1827. Until her husband put a stop to it Sophia taught Douglass the alphabet. Between 1829 and 1830 He later received lessons from white playmates while working in the Auld & Harrison ship yard. Ibid., 231–232.
64. Douglass (1846), quoted in Blassingame, *The Frederick Douglass Papers*, 1: 346–347.
65. Douglass, *My Bondage*, 160, 299.
66. As shown Douglass's formative influences were mainly African. Consider his comments during the time he was forced to part with Betsy Bailey: "I look back to this as among the heaviest of my childhood's sorrows. My grandmother! My grandmother! And the little hut, and the joyous *circle* under her care, but especially she, who made us sorry when she left us but for an hour, and glad on her return,—how could I leave her and the good old home?" see Douglass, *My Bondage*, 143–144.
67. Ibid., 181. [Italics Mine].
68. Harriet Jacobs, *Incidents in the Life of A Slave Girl* (1861; repr.; New York and London: Norton, 2001).
69. Ibid., 309.
70. Douglass (1845), quoted in Blassingame, *The Frederick Douglass Papers*, 1: 32–33.
71. Douglass (1848), quoted in Blassingame, *The Frederick Douglass Papers*, 2: 130–131.
72. Douglass felt that "it was in vain that the pulpit of St. Michael's had constantly inculcated these plausible doctrines. Nature laughed them to corn." Douglass, *My Bondage*, 306.
73. Douglass, *Narrative*, 72, 78.
74. Douglass, *My Bondage*, 301–302.
75. See Douglass, *Narrative*, 70–73; Douglass, *My Bondage*, 298–300. Three years later in 1838 Douglass escaped slavery. Shortly after he reached the free state of New York he was married to Anna Murray by James W. C. Pennington, a Presbyterian minister and fellow escaped slave from Maryland. Anna

Murray was a free black woman from Caroline County. Towards the end of the year he and his wife relocated to New Bedford, Massachusetts where he found work as caulker. The couple preferred to worship with a black congregation rather than attend a church that maintained a mixed constituency. They found that the latter had the tendency to segregate its black attendees. Consequently, Douglass and Anna became active members in the New Bedford Zion Methodist Church. It was there around other blacks that they felt most comfortable. Douglass, *My Bondage*, 360–362.

76. Douglass, *Narrative*, 68.
77. Ibid., 97.
78. Douglass, *My Bondage*, 98.
79. Ibid.
80. Ibid., 17–18. For a discussion on "the Hamitic curse" and its implications for eighteenth and nineteenth-century slaves see Michael Gomez, *Reversing Sail: A History of the African Diaspora* (Cambridge: Cambridge University Press, 2005) 21–22.
81. *The Frederick Douglass Papers*, Blassingame, ed., 2.
82. *Frederick Douglass Papers*, Blassingame, ed.
83. Ibid., 407.
84. Douglass (1848), quoted in Blassingame, *The Frederick Douglass Papers*, 2: 130.
85. For Patrick Rael, *Black Identity & Black Protest in the Antebellum North* (Chapell Hill and London, 2002)
86. Stephen Butterfield, *Black Autobiography in America* (Amherst: University of Massachusetts Press, 1974) 15–16, 30, 52.
87. Nathaniel P. Rogers (1844), quoted in Blassingame, *The Frederick Douglass Papers*, 1: 26–27.

NOTES TO CHAPTER 2

1. J. Noel Heermance and William Farrison were the first to publish extensive treatments on Brown in the late 1960s. Heermance did not give any attention to Brown's observations on African culture and Farrison argued that he was at best "half amused" with it. L. H. Welchel Jr. and drew similar conclusions in the mid-eighties. J. Noel Heermance, *William Wells Brown and Clotelle: A Portrait of the Artist in the First Negro Novel* (Shoe String, 1969); William Farrison, *William Wells Brown: Author & Reformer* (Chicago: University of Chicago, 1969), 45; L. H. Welchel Jr., *My Chains Fell Off: William Wells Brown, Fugitive Abolitionist* (Lanham: University Press of America, 1985), 5. In each of their works Paul Jefferson and William Andrews were not interested in examining Brown's cultural connections to Africa. Paul Jefferson, eds., *The Travels of William Wells Brown* (New York: Markus Wiener, 1991); William Andrews, *From Fugitive Slave to Free man: The Autobiographies of William Wells Brown* (Columbia: University of Missouri Press, 2003).
2. William Wells Brown, *The Rising Son; or, The Antecedents and Advancement of the Colored Race* (Boston: A. G. Brown, 1874; repr.; Florida: Mnemosyne Inc., 1969), 94–95. Here one is reminded of Douglass's recollection of hearing "a wild hoarse laugh arise from a circle and often a song." Frederick Douglass, "My Bondage and My Freedom" (1855; repr.; in *Douglass Autobiographies*, New York: Penguin, 1994), 188, [Italics mine]. Laughter is also associated with circular dance in Thomas Higginson's observations of the practice in the Sea Islands. Thomas Wentworth Higginson, *Army Life in a Black Regiment* (New York: W. W. Norton, 1984), 41 (originally published in 1869).

3. Brown, *The Rising Son*, 95. [Italics mine]. Jack Tattnall of Wilmington Island Georgia similarly disclosed that "at duh fewnul wen we beat duh drum we mahch roun duh grabe in a ring." Georgia Writer's Project, *Drums and Shadows*, (Georgia: The University of Georgia Press), 107.

4. Brown, *The Rising Son*, 95–96.

5. Ibid., 94.

6. Brown, *My Southern Home: Or, The South and Its People* (Boston: 1880; repr., New Jersey: The Gregg Press, 1968), 69.

7. Ibid., 121–122. For a broader discussion on the significance of country marks among West Africans see Michael Gomez, *Exchanging Our Country Marks: The Transformation of African Identity in the Colonial and Antebellum South* (Chapel Hill: University of North Carolina Press, 1998).

8. Brown, *My Southern Home*, 121–124.

9. Ibid., 191. W.E.B. Dubois claimed, "Those who have thus not witnessed the frenzy of a Negro revival in the untouched backwoods of the South can but dimly realize the religious feeling of the slave." W.E.B. Dubois, *The Souls of Black Folk*, in John Hope Franklin, ed., *Three Negro Classics* (New York: Avon Books, 1963), 338 (originally published in 1903).

10. Farrison, 363, 440.

11. William Wells Brown, *Narrative of William W. Brown, a Fugitive Slave, Written by Himself* (Boston: 1847), 91–93. At least eight editions of this narrative have been published. The text focuses on the first twenty years of Brown's life. The content is generally consistent throughout all the editions. References to the narrative here rely on the first edition which has been reprinted in William Loren Katz, *Five Slave Narratives*, ed. (New York: Arno, 1968). Brown might have been inspired by Frederick Douglass's narrative to publish his own life story just two years later. Brown's *Narrative* enjoyed a wide readership selling over three thousand copies in the first six months of its publication. Due to such a high demand for the text, four editions totaling ten thousand copies were published in two years. See Farrison, 113–114. It should also be noted that the term "uncle" calls to mind our discussion of African etiquette concerning Frederick Douglass's narrative. See Douglass, *Life and Times of Frederick Douglass* (1893; repr.; *Douglass Autobiographies*, New York: Penguin, 1994), 490.

12. Brown, *Narrative*, 93.

13. William Wells Brown, *Clotel; or, The President's Daughter. With a Sketch of the Author's Life* (London, 1853; repr.; in Henry Louis Gates, Jr., ed., *Three Classic African-American Novels* (New York: Vintage Classics, 1990). The story essentially revolves around the trials and tribulations of Currer, a mulatto slave from Virginia and her quadroon daughters Clotel and Athesa. Scholars have generally focused on the various facets of the interracial relationship between Clotel and her white slave owner Horatio.

14. See Heermance.

15. Brown, *Narrative*, 93.

16. Farrison, 297–298. William Wells Brown, *The Escape; Or, A Leap For Freedom: A Drama in Five Acts* (Boston: Robert F. Wallcut, 1858; repr.; Knoxville: University of Tennessee, 2001).

17. Brown, *The Escape*, 29. Melinda's response to Dr. Gaines calls to mind Theophus Smith's discussion of the conjure doctor's desire to harm a person through the invocation of exceptional powers. Theophus H. Smith, *Conjuring Culture* (New York and Oxford: Oxford U Press, 1994), 4.

18. Farrison, 297–298.

19. William Wells Brown, *The Black Man, His Antecedents, His Genius, and His Achievements* (New York and Boston, 1863; repr.; New York: Arno Press, 1969), 59.

20. Farrison, 367; Brown, *The Black Man*, 35.
21. It is possible that Brown may have drawn on Thomas R. Gray's *The Confessions of Nat Turner, the Leader of the Late Insurrection in Southampton, VA*. Farrison, 338–339.
22. Brown, *The Black Man*, 59–63. It is significant that Brown saw a relationship between conjuring, fortune-telling, and dreams. While each were distinctly different cultural expressions of the African American religious experience, they all functioned to affect change through ritually patterned behavior. See Theophus Smith's definition of conjuring culture. Smith, *Conjuring Culture*, 6.
23. Ibid., 71.
24. Brown, Ibid., 75.
25. Brown, *The Rising Son*, 110.
26. Ibid., 111.
27. Ibid.
28. James M. Phillippo, *Jamaica, Past and Present* (London: J. Snow, 1843).
29. Brown, *The Rising Son*, 252.
30. Ibid., 253.
31. William Wells Brown, *My Southern Home: or, The South and Its People*, 59–60. In this work Brown took the literary liberty to provide his actual observations of what he observed and heard while he was in slavery. Many of the themes and illustrations overlap with his other writings.
32. Ibid.
33. Brown, *My Southern Home*, 70. Brown commented on the spiritual importance of reptiles among the Dahomey natives. "On certain days," he writes "they are taken out by the priests or doctors, and paraded about the streets, the bearers allowing them to coil themselves around their arms, necks, and bodies." They were also used as truth-telling aids. The bite of a person in question was proof of their guilt. See Brown, *Rising Son*, 108. Major Arthur Glyn Lenard found that such practices were more than simply a form of Ophiolatry among nineteenth-century Nigerians. It was often believed that the spirit of one's ancestor dwelled within the reptile and if treated well could protect its bearer. He writes "Reptiles, snakes, and crocodiles particularly are much more utilized as emblems, simply, it is to be presumed, because they are more in evidence in the forests and rivers of the Delta than any other species of animals, consequently must have appealed to the natives as the most convenient and suitable repositories for the ancestral manes." Major Arthur Glyn Leonard, *The Lower Niger and Its Tribes* (New York: The Macmillan Co., 1906), 317. John Pearce describes a similar practice in Africa where "Juju bags containing graveyard dirt and other material which had a spell put upon it by juju are effective for either good or evil purposes. A bag of this sort worn around the neck, as a Catholic wears a scapula, serves as a protection from the spells of enemies. However, if a man wishes to work evil on his enemy, he may purchase a juju bag containing evil powder, and through it cast a spell on his enemy." See Georgia Writers' Project, *Drums and Shadows*, 202.
34. Brown, *My Southern Home*, 70, 71.
35. Ibid., 77.
36. Ibid., 78–79.
37. Ibid., 10–11. Describing the role of the African-American root doctor or conjurer, Puckett writes: "Some . . . burn a kind of powder called "goopher dust," which represents the person being hoodooed . . . this causes the conjured individual to lose his personality and to become sick or insane. One must have the power to make up a protecting "hand" or charm. Another

conjurer or hoodo outside the vicinity can work a cure for one so afflicted."
Newbell Niles Puckett, *Folk Beliefs of The Southern Negro* (Chapel Hill:
The University of North Carolina Press, 1926), 215.

38. Jacob Stroyer's narrative *My Life in the South* and the story of John Warren
included in Benjamin Drew's collection of mini slave narratives of those who
fled to Canada also contain descriptions of goopher use. Stroyer was born a
slave in 1849 in an area southeast of Columbia, South Carolina. He was freed
when the war ended. By the age of twenty he was already a licensed preacher of
the A.M.E. church and he later became a deacon in Rhode Island. His account
reflects the persistence of African values into both the black ministerial and
slave class. Stroyer said that the slaves had three ways of detecting thieves. The
first method, which could only take place under the cover of night, entailed
using the bible as a sort of charm. Four men would visit the residences of the
slaves with a string attached to the Bible and if the holy book flipped around
they had found their culprit. The second method was the same as the first only
they used a sieve instead of the bible. According to Stroyer the last and "truest"
way of finding thieves was passed down from one generation to the next. It was
believed that a person would be most truthful when the time came for them to
die. They feared that if they were not truthful at this moment they would be
tormented in the spirit world. Thus, they were convinced that "graveyard dust"
mixed with water would yield the absolute truth. The examining committee
collected the dirt of the person who had last died. If those in question stole from
someone it was believed that they would die from drinking the truth serum.
Since none wanted to experience despair in their afterlife the *truth* always came
out. Jacob Stroyer, "My Life in the South" (1885; repr.; in William Loren Katz,
ed., *Five Slave Narratives*, New York: Arno, 1969), 58–59. John Warren was
from Wilson County Tennessee and spent some of his slave years in Marshall
County Mississippi. He, like Brown's companion Dinkie, also knew how to
remove the scent of animals with graveyard dirt. When dog catchers chased
him during the times he took flight he would retrieve the soiled dust of a person
that had been buried a long time, combine it with water and cover parts of his
body and his immediate surroundings. This assured that the dogs would not
follow. Benjamin Drew, "The Refugee: A North-Side View of Slavery" (1855;
repr.; *Four Fugitive Slave Narratives*, with an introduction by Robin Winks
(Massachusetts: Addison-Wesley, 1969), 130.

39. Ibid., 60.
40. Ibid., 61.
41. Brown, *My Southern Home*, 155.
42. Ibid., 153–157. The reference to "shout" strongly suggests that this was the
ring shout ceremony.
43. Ibid.
44. Ibid., 157. One is reminded of the "caul" or the gift of second sight. See *Drums
and Shadows* that points to the following sources which describe the caul or the
gift of second sight; Martha Beckwith, *Black Roadways* (Chapel Hill: The University of North Carolina Press, 1929); Melville Herskovits, *Life in a Haitian
Valley* (New York and London: Knoph, 1937).
45. Brown, *My Southern Home*, 158. For a discussion of "signs" in Africa consult
Richard Burton, *A Mission to Gelele, King of Dahomey* (London: Tinsley Bro-
thres, 1864); and A. B. Ellis, *The Yoruba-Speaking Peoples of the Slave Coast
of West Africa* (London: Chapman & Hall, 1890). Warren Beckwith explores
similar beliefs held by Jamaicans, *Black Roadways* (Chapel Hill: The University of North Carolina Press, 1929). Brown's descriptions of *signs* closely mirror
those found in Arna Bontemps' seminal novel *Black Thunder*. After combing
through Fisk University's collection of slave narratives, Bontemps, a literary son

of the Harlem Renaissance, was inspired to write a historical novel of the actual 1800 Virginia slave conspiracy led by Gabriel Prosser. It is hard not to imagine that he often had the writings of Brown in mind when he wrote the book at his parents' house in the Watts community of Los Angeles. Able to interweave African cultural aspects of slave resistance into their texts both authors showed how slaves read the *signs*. In Bontemps' story the plan begins to unravel when two co-conspirators decide to undermine the scheme by exposing the secret and Gabriel fails to follow the warning of the *signs* while concurrently neglecting to engage in the kind of African ritual that Toussaint was said to have practiced in the San Domingo uprising. Most of the slaves chose not to abandon African folkways. Juba, Gabriel's loyal aide and companion, acquired a protective amulet for Gabriel with the hope that it would avert any malice directed towards him in the form of negative conjure. Similarly, Brown tells us that among St. Louis slaves "there was a general belief that a horse-shoe hung over the door would insure good luck. I have seen negroes, otherwise comparatively intelligent, refuse to pick up a pin, needle, or other such object, dropped by a negro, because, as they alleged, if the person who dropped the articles had a spite against them, to touch anything they dropped would voudou them, and make them seriously ill." For this, a protective hand was believed to be able to cure this affliction. See Brown, *My Southern Home*, 69. When Bontemps' characters were troubled by a fierce thunderstorm on the night of the planned revolt and the dreadful omen of birds entering homes, a good number of the conspirators tried to convince Gabriel that they were "scairt of the signs" and perhaps this meant that this it was not the best time to strike. Though he was well aware of the *signs* he would not heed to any them. He believed there was no better time for them to own their freedom. Yet, his decision to pay no attention to the warnings and reject Juba's charm proved fatal. When authorities did eventually apprehend the stubborn leader he admitted "the stars was against, though; that's all." For Brown's non-fictional characters then, the "signs" served to assure the slaves that emancipation was near. On the other hand, the individuals in Arna Bontemps' novel mentioned above were for the most part quite concerned with the "signs" to which they came face to face. Brown, a leading abolitionist, and Bontemps, a fine student of the slave narrative, were able to capture the balance of "good" and "evil" that was endemic to the interpretation of "signs." Arna Bontemps, *Black Thunder* (1936), repr.; (Boston: Beacon, 1968), 211.

46. Like Frederick Douglass, Brown noted that planters generally spent little or no time tending to the religious needs of slaves and those who did preached a gospel that sanctioned their subordination. William Wells Brown, *My Southern Home: or, The South and Its People* (A. G. Brown, 1880; repr.; New Jersey: The Gregg Press, 1968), 3.; William Wells Brown, *The Rising Son*, 90–91.

47. William Wells Brown, "Narrative of William, A Fugitive Slave" (Boston: 1847), repr.; ed. *William Loren Katz, Five Slave Narratives* (New York: Arno, 1968), 27.

48. Ibid.

49. Ibid., 29–31.

50. Ibid., 66.

51. Ibid., 70.

52. Ibid., 73.

53. Ibid., 56–57.

54. Brown, *Narrative*, 37–40.

55. Ibid., 83–84; Luke 12: 47.

56. Ibid., 52. Brown explored this matter in his novel *Clotelle*. Uncle Tony was a slave who resided with Clotelle on the estate of Mrs. Miller. Brown described

Uncle Tony as a very religious man who could often be heard praying "O Lord, thou knows that the white folks are not Christians, but the black people are God's own children." William Wells Brown, *Clotelle; or, The President's Daughter: A Narrative of Slave Life in the United States* (London, 1853; repr.; in J. Noel Heermance, 42.

57. *The Black Abolitionist Papers*, ed. C. Peter Ripley (Chapel Hill: University of North Carolina, 1985–1992): IV (1847–1858), 245.
58. Brown, 82–84.
59. Ibid., 54.
60. Brown, *Clotelle*, 103.
61. Ibid., 58.
62. Ibid., 58, 65.
63. Ibid.
64. Brown, *Narrative*, 17–20
65. Brown, *Clotelle*, 39.
66. See Douglass, "My Bondage and My Freedom" (1855; repr.; in *Douglass Autobiographies*, New York: Penguin, 1994), 181.
67. Brown, *Clotelle*, 66.
68. Brown, *The Black Man*, 46.
69. In 1861 Brown began to promote Haitian immigration on the basis that, unlike the design of the American Colonization Society, the plan of resettling blacks in Haiti was voluntary. He believed that Haiti could give blacks an opportunity to participate in the building of a strong republic and become successful landowners and farmers. See Farrison, 334–336.
70. Brown, *The Black Man*, 59.
71. Ibid., 75–85.
72. Ibid., 122; See William Wells Brown, *The Anti-Slavery Harp: A Collection of Songs for Anti-Slavery Meetings* (Boston: Bela Marsh, 1848).
73. Ibid., 96.
74. Ibid., 105.
75. Ibid., 125.
76. Ibid., 140.
77. Farrison, 77–78.
78. Ibid., 79.
79. Ibid., 310–311.
80. Brown, *The Black Man*, 150.
81. Ibid., 150–151. Brown omitted the source of the passage. Brown also had a tumultuous relationship with Martin Delany. Nevertheless, Brown included a succinct passage on Delany in *The Black Man* in which he expressed his regard for Delany's oratory abilities. In concluding his thoughts on Delany Brown wrote, "Devotedly attached to his fatherland, he goes for a 'Negro Nationality.' Whatever he undertakes, he executes it with all the powers that God has given him; and what would appear as an obstacle in the way of other men, would be brushed aside by Martin R. Delany." Brown, *The Black Man*, 175. For a discussion on the rapport between Brown and Delany see Farrison, 344–345.
82. Brown, *The Rising Son*, 326.4
83. Brown, *My Southern Home*, 242.

NOTES TO CHAPTER 3

1. Theophus H. Smith, *Conjuring Culture: Biblical Formations of Black America* (New York and Oxford: Oxford University Press, 1994), 38.

2. The term "Mosaic" is borrowed from Smith, 35.

3. Smith's analysis of Tubman's relationship to Moses is limited to her efforts on the Underground Railroad. Ibid., 69.

4. Jean M. Humez, *Harriet Tubman: The Life and the Life Stories* (Madison: The University of Wisconsin Press, 2003); Kate C. Larson, *Bound For The Promise Land: Harriet Tubman, Portrait of An American Hero* (New York: Random House, 2004); Catherine Clinton, *Harriet Tubman: The Road to Freedom* (New York and Boston: Little, Brown and Company, 2004).

5. Earl Conrad, *Harriet Tubman* (Washington, D.C.: The Associated Publishers, 1943).

6. Larson, xv, 305 n3.

7. Franklin Sanborn, "Harriet Tubman," *The Commonwealth*, Boston July 17 (1863); Ednah Dow Littlehale Cheney, "Moses," *Freedmen's Record*, March 1865; Sarah H. Bradford, *Scenes in the Life of Harriet Tubman* (Auburn, New York: W.J. Moses, 1869); Bradford, *Harriet Tubman, the Moses of Her People* (1886; repr.; Bedford, Mass.; Applewood Books, 1993).

8. Humez, 6.

9. Larson, 46–47.

10. Bradford, 23.

11. Cheney, 36. See also Humez, 212.

12. As mentioned in my first chapter on Frederick Douglass, given what Bishop Daniel Payne had to say about the ring shout in Maryland it would not have been out of the ordinary for Tubman to observe the ceremony there. Daniel Payne, *Recollections of Seventy Years* (1888; repr., New York: Arno Press, 1968), 254–256.

13. Ibid., 76.

14. W.E.B. DuBois, *The Souls of Black Folk* (New York: Washington Square Press, 1970), 155.

15. Ibid., 83–84.

16. Bradford., 61–65.

17. Ibid.

18. Ibid.

19. Exodus 7:10. This Scripture indicates that God commanded Moses to change Pharaoh's rod to a serpent.

20. There were other times when Tubman seemed to enjoy duping her masters: "Sometimes, when she and her party were concealed in the woods, they saw their pursuers pass, on their horses, down the high road, tacking up the advertisements for them on the fences and trees. 'And then how we laughed,' said she. 'We was the foos, and they was the wise men, but we wasn't fools enough to go down the high road in the broad daylight.'" (Bradford, 1869, 25). Humez reveals some of Tubman's other trickster tales during her rescue efforts. These include pinching chickens to distract her master; acting as if she was able to read to frustrate slave catchers who knew she was illiterate; taking a train south to throw her pursuers off course; and singing songs to throw off those questioning her. Humez, 189.

21. Bradford, 74; Exodus 14: 21–31.

22. Ibid., 85.

23. Ibid., 86–87.

24. Ibid., 87.

25. Ibid., 81.

26. Ibid., 83, 87.

27. For the relationship that Tubman had with William Seward see Humez, 26–27.

28. Humez, 258.

29. William Wells Brown, *The Rising Son; or, The Antecedents and Advancement of the Colored Race* (Boston: A.G. Brown, 1874; repr.; Florida: Mnemosyne Inc., 1969), 538.

30. Thomas Wentworth Higginson noted that spirituals sung by his black soldiers were largely drawn from the Old Testament's Books of Moses. "Most of the great events of the past, down to the period of the American Revolution," he observed, "they instinctively attribute to Moses." Thomas Wentworth Higginson, *Army Life in a Black Regiment* (1869; Beacon Press ed., Boston, 1962), 205. A northern chaplain visiting Alabama in 1865 recorded of the slaves, "Moses is their ideal of all that is high, and noble, and perfect, in man," while Christ was thought of "not so much in the light of a *spiritual Deliverer*, as that of a second Moses." Quoted in Peter Kolchin, *First Freedom: The Responses of Alabama's Blacks to Emancipation and Reconstruction* (Westport, Conn.: Greenwood Press, 1972), 118. For this reference also see Lawrence W. Levine *Black Culture and Black Consciousness: Afro-American Folk Thought from Slavery to Freedom* (New York: Oxford University Press, 1977), 50. Levine's work makes clear that Moses was a significant figure in the slaves' songs. Of one spiritual he writes, "the slaves rehearsed the triumphs of the Hebrew Children in verse after verse, concluding each with the comforting thought: 'And the God dat lived in Moses' [Dan'el's, David's] time is jus' de same today.' The 'mighty rocky road' that 'I must travel,' another of the slaves' songs insisted, is 'De rough rocky road what Moses done travel.'" Levine explains that "these songs state as clearly as anything can the manner in which the sacred world of the slaves was able to fuse the precedents of the past, the conditions of the present, and the promise of the future into one connected reality." Levine, 51.

31. Zora Neale Hurston, *Mules and Men* (1935; repr.; New York: Harper & Row, 1990), 183–84. See Smith for additional commentary on this, 32–33.

32. Ibid., 184.

33. Harry Middleton Hyatt, *Hoodoo-Conjuration-Witchcraft-Rootwork: Beliefs Accepted by Many Negroes and White Persons, These Being Orally Recorded among Blacks and Whites*, vol. 2 of 5 (Hannibal, Mo.: Western Publishing Co., 1970, 1755–1758. For a larger discussion on the *Seven Books of Moses* in the African-American folk tradition see Migene Gonza'lez-Wippler, *The New Revised Sixth and Seventh Books of Moses and the Magical Uses of the Psalms* (New York: Original Publications, 1991), 5.

34. Rosa Belle Holt, "A Heroine in Ebony" in *Chautauquan* 23, (1886), 459–462. Also quoted in Humez, 260.

35. Exodus, 4.

36. Ibid., 115. It is not known if Tubman ever forecasted the weather like her father, but she claims to have once prophesized an earthquake. Bradford writes, "She woke from a sleep one day in great agitation, and ran to the houses of her colored neighbors, exclaiming that a 'dreadful thing was happening somewhere, the ground was opening, and the houses were falling in, and the people being killed faster then they was in the war—faster than they was in the war.' At that very time, or near it, an earthquake was occurring in the northern part of South America, for the telegram came that day, though why a vision of it should be sent to Harriet no one can divine." (Humez, 259, Bradford, 147–148).

37. Zora Neal Hurston, *Moses: Man of the Mountain* (1939; repr.; New Jersey: Chatham Bookseller, 1967). See also Smith, 33, 49 n.37.

38. Ibid., 119.

39. Ibid., 120.

40. Ibid., 25–30.

41. Ibid., 115.
42. Of the total number of imports that disembarked in what became the United States at least 13% embarked from the Bight of Biafra, David Eltis, Stephen D. Behrendt, David Richardson, and Herbert Klein eds., *The Trans-Atlantic Slave Trade: A Database on CD-Rom* (Cambridge: University Press, 1999). For a discussion of the Igbo presence in America see Gomez, 115. There is evidence to suggest that the notion of flying Africans would not have been lost on the Akan. Commenting on this phenomenon among the Akan Anthony Ephirim-Donkor explains that "the Akan people also believe that the soul can be put to flight (*ne kra eguan*)." This would happen when one is incarcerated. Since slavery is a form of incarceration it makes sense that some of the Akan who ended up in the Americas held on to this belief. Anthony Ephirim-Donkor, *African Spirituality: On Becoming Ancestors* (New Jersey: Africa World Press, 1997), 73.
43. Bradford, *Scenes*, 55–56. See also Humez, 260–261.
44. Georgia Writers Project, 28.
45. Hurston, *Mules and Men*, 184–85. See also Smith, 33.
46. Humez, 188.
47. Cheney, 36. See also Humez, 235–236.
48. Bradford, *Scenes*, 24–25. See also Humez, 236.
49. Zora Neale Hurston, *Tell My Horse: Voodoo and Life in Haiti and Jamaica* (1938; repr.; New York: Harper and Row, 1990), 116. Hurston informs us that Damballah is also spelled Damballa and Dambala. Michael Gomez suggests that Da or Dan Bada, the supreme deity of the Fon of Dahomey (contemporary Benin), became Damballah of Haiti and Louisiana. *Exchanging Our Country Marks: The Transformation of African Identities in the Colonial and Antebellum South* (Chapel Hill: University of North Carolina Press, 1998), 57.
50. Hurston, *Tell My Horse*, 116.
51. Ibid., 118.
52. Larson, 156.
53. Ibid., 156–158.
54. Bradford, 118.
55. See David S. Reynolds, *John Brown, Abolitionist: The Man Who Killed Slavery, Sparked the Civil War, and Seeded Civil Rights* (New York: Knopf, 2005).
56. Ibid., 119.
57. Larson, 176.
58. See Jean M. Humez's *Harriet Tubman: the Life and the Life Stories*, a new monograph on Tubman in which the author considers Tubman's role as a gifted story orator on her life story. 133.
59. Cheney, 36–37.
60. *The Voice of The Fugitive*, a newspaper edited by Tubman's contemporary Henry Bibb, also included an article on the sacred snakes of Whydah, Dahomey. See also Paul Erdmann Isert, *Letters On West Africa And The Slave Trade: Paul Erdmann Isert's Journey to Guinea and the Caribbean Islands in Columbia* (New York: Oxford University Press, 1992), 128; Harold Courlander, *A Treasury of African Folklore: The Oral Literature, Traditions, Myths, Legends, Epics, Tales, Recollections, Wisdom, Sayings, and Humor of Africa* (New York: Crown Publishers, 1975), 284–285, 420, 435–437, 506.
61. Georgia Writer's Project, *Drums and Shadows* (Georiga: Univeristy of Georgia Press, 1940), 26.
62. Major Arthur Glyn Leonard, *The Lower Niger and Its Tribes* (New York: Macmillan, 1987), 147.
63. Georgia Writer's Project, 77.
64. Ibid., 83.

65. Ibid., 14.
66. Ibid., 24.
67. Smith, 38.
68. She supported herself by washing, cooking, sewing and running an eatery for soldiers in Beaufort.
69. Bradford, 95–98.
70. Hurston, *Moses*, 64.
71. Larson, 210–213.
72. Bradford, 101.
73. Ibid., 102.
74. Ibid., 104. See Georgia Writers Project, *Drums and Shadows* for further commentary on nightly funeral rituals, 182, 192.
75. Bradford, 105.
76. Courlander, 200. See also Georgia Writers Project, *Drums and Shadows* for further commentary on nightly funeral rituals, 182, 192.
77. *Drums and Shadows*, 141.
78. Bradford, 92.
79. Ibid., 93.
80. Larson, 109
81. Ibid., 283.
82. Larson, 45.

NOTES TO CHAPTER 4

1. Harriet Jacobs, *Incidents in the Life of a Slave Girl [by] Linda Brent*. (New York: Harcourt Brace Jovanovich, 1973). See also Harriet Jacobs, *Incidents in the Life of a Slave Girl: Contexts and Criticisms*. Ed. by Nellie Y. Mckay and Frances Smith Foster. (New York and London: W.W. Norton & Company, 2001), xv. References to Jacobs's narrative in this chapter rely on this edition.
2. Jacobs, xiii-xv.
3. Ibid., xvi-xxii; Harriet Jacobs, *Incidents* (Cambridge: Harvard University Press, 1987). Ed. by Jean Yellin.
4. See *Incidents* Harvard University Press 2000 edition, with Introduction by Jean Yellin; Jean Yellin, *Harriet Jacobs: A Life* (New York: Basic Civitas Books, 2004).
5. Karen Beardslee, "Through Slave Culture's Lens Comes the Abundant Source: Harriet A. Jacobs's Incidents in the Life of a Slave Girl"—Critical Essay in *Melus* (Spring, 1999).
6. Jean Yellin, "Written by Herself: Harriet Jacobs' Slave Narrative," in *American Literature* 53.3, (November, 1981): 379–486; Jacobs, *Incidents*, Harvard 2000 edition, xv; Nellie Y. Mckay profiles the life of Jacobs and two other black women from different time periods who all overcame the struggles of gender norms. Nellie Y. Mckay, "The Girls Who Became the Women: Childhood Memories in the Autobiographies of Harriet Jacobs, Mary Church Terrell, and Anne Moody," in Florence Howe, ed., *Tradition and the Talents of Women* (Urbana and Chicago: U of Illinois Press, 1991), 106–24; Nell Irvin Painter investigates the ways in which Jacobs's text is a testimony of the ways in which black women were faced with the challenge of race, gender, and class. Nell Irvin Painter, "Three Southern Women and Freud: A Non-Exceptionalist Approach to Race, Class, and Gender in the Slave South," in Ann-Louise, ed., *Feminists Revision History* (New Brunswick: Rutgers UP, 1994), 195–216. Michelle Burnahm explores Jacobs's ability to conceal her discussion of sexual

exploitation in plain view. Michelle Burnham, "Loopholes of Resistance: Harriet Jacobs' Slave Narrative and the Critique of Agency in Foucault," in *Arizona Quarterly* 49.2, (summer 1993): 53–73; Sandra Gunning reasons that Jacobs sought to express herself through the language of domesticity because it was the popular genre of the time through which she could be heard. Gunning argues that the authenticating documents in the text do not prevent Jacobs's voice from being heard. Sandra Gunning, "Reading and Redemption in *Incidents in the Life of a Slave Girl*," in Deborah M. Garfield and Rafia Zafar eds., *Harriet Jacobs and Incidents in the Life of a Slave Girl: New Critical Essays* (New York: Cambridge UP, 1996), 131–154.

7. Jacobs, 65.
8. Ibid., 11.
9. Ibid., 13.
10. Ibid., 26, 35, 91.
11. Ibid., 65.
12. Jacobs explained that, "They send the Bible to heathen abroad, and neglect the heathen at home. I am glad that missionaries go out to the dark corners of the earth; but I ask them not to overlook the dark corners at home." Ibid., 61–62.
13. Ibid., 14–15.
14. Of her initial religious impressions of Steventon England Jacobs says, "My visit to England is a memorable event in my life, from the fact of my having there received strong religious impressions. The contemptuous manner in which the communion had been administered to colored people, in my native place; the church membership of Dr. Flint, and others like him; and the buying and selling of slaves, by professed ministers of the gospel, had given me a prejudice against the Episcopal church. The whole service seemed to me a mockery and sham. But my home in Steventon was in the family of a clergyman, who was a true disciple of Jesus. The beauty of his daily life inspired me with faith in the genuineness of Christian professions. Grace entered my heart, and I knelt at the communion table, I trust, in true humility of soul." Ibid., 143.
15. Ibid., 57.
16. Jacobs, 60. Douglass was amazed to meet northerners who were convinced that singing of slaves meant that they were content. He writes: "It is impossible to conceive of a greater mistake. Slaves sing most when they are most unhappy. The songs of the slave represent the sorrows of his heart: and he is relieved by them, only as an aching heart is relieved by tears." Douglass, *Narrative*, 24.
17. Jacobs, 58. For further mention of coffee grounds as means to reveal the future see Newbell Niles Puckett, *Folk Beliefs of the Southern Negro*, (New York: Dover, 1969), 355. *Drums and Shadows* provides an account of a root doctor from Brownville, Georgia who was also born with the power to foretell the future through the use of coffee ground: "I kin use leaves an coffe grouns an a suttn kine uh seed known as duh sensitive aw jumpin seed. Yuh fine deze seeds at suttn times long duh sho uh duh Wes Indies. uh hab tuh keep duh seeds in a closed containuh aw dey will jis disappeah. Tuh Tell fawchuns you spread duh seeds out fo yuh on duh groun an dey'll moob bout. Dey mob cawdn tuh wut yuh tinkin. Tellin fawchuns is jis a mattuh uh concentratin yuh imagination on suttn tings. Den ebryting will appeah fo yuh." Georgia Writer's Project, *Drums and Shadows* (Athens: University of Georgia, 1940), 58. Various kinds of seeds were also used to reveal the future in various parts of West Africa. In Dahomey, for example, individuals who

told future used palm kernels. Melville Herskovits, *Dahomey* (New York: J. J. Augustin, 1938), vol. 11, 209, 210.

18. In the previous chapters fortunetellers and conjure doctors have been identified in the slave narratives of Frederick Douglass, William Wells Brown, and Harriet Tubman. Henry Bibb, a former slave from Kentucky who became well known for his abolitionist efforts which included encouraging fugitives to settle in Canada, also wrote of his experiences with conjure doctors. In a recent introduction to Bibb's narrative Charles Heglar concluded that the author "deflates and dismisses the love charms of the conjurers." Yet Bibb admitted to having a firm belief in conjuration while he was held in slavery. When slaves desired to avert the maltreatment of their masters Bibb says they often relied on "some kind of bitter root" whose effectiveness depended on the person receiving the medicine accurately spitting the concoction towards their afflicter. Another remedy entailed scattering special powders around the victim's residence. One prescription included alum and salt. Red pepper, cow dung and "white people's hair" served as another remedy. When Bibb sought the advice of local conjure doctors to win the affection of two love interests he was instructed to rub the bone of a bullfrog on the woman he desired and to wear a lock of the women's hair in his shoes. According to Bibb such beliefs and practices were held by "the great masses of southern slaves. It is given to them by tradition, and can never be erased." Henry Bibb, *The Life and Adventures of Henry Bibb: An American Slave*, with an introduction by Charles Heglar (New York: 1849; repr.; Madison: University of Wisconsin, 2001), 25–32.

19. Jacobs's allusion to the slaves' "invisible church" calls to mind Simon Brown's remarks on the distinction between slave religion and that of the master class which he observed in Virginia. Brown says: "The fact is, the black folk in my day didn't even have a church. They meet in a cabin in the cole weather an' outdoors, under a tree or a "brush arbor" in the summer time. Sometimes the Massa's preacher would "talk" at the mettins 'bout bein' obedient to our massas an' good servants, an ' b'out goin' to heaven when we die.' . . . But, oh, my, when my people got together to "Wishop" (Worship) God, the Spirit would "move in the meetin!" William John Faulkner, *The Days When the Animals Talked* (Chicago: Follette Publishers, 1977), 52–59. See also Sterling Stuckey, *Slave Culture*, 33.

20. Ibid., 58.

21. Lydia Parrish, *Slave Songs of the Georgia Sea Islands* (New York: Creative Age Press, 1942), 54.

22. For a discussion of slave culture in the North see Stuckey, *Slave Culture*, 73–83.

23. Jacobs, 74. Jacobs's consultation with her parents before she escapes calls to mind Douglass's meeting with Sandy prior to his escape. Douglass, *My Bondage*, 286, 309.

24. Stuckey, *Slave Culture*, 25, 39–43.

25. Jacobs, 115.

26. See interview with John Pearce in Georgia Writers Project, *Drums and Shadows*, 196.

27. George Thomas Basden, *Among the Ibos of Nigeria* (Philadelphia: J.B. Lippincott Co., 1931), 115–116. For additional treatments of similar beliefs see also William Bosman, *Description of the Coast of Guinea*: (London: F. Knapton, 1705), 232; C. K. Meek, *Law and Authority in a Nigerian Tribe* (London: Oxford University Pess, 1937), 309; Robert Hamill Nassau, *Fetichism in West Africa* (New York: Charles Scribner's Sons, 1904), 228.

28. Douglass, *My Bondage*, 163.

29. James W.C. Pennington, "The Fugitive Blacksmith, in Arna Bontemps, ed., *Great Slave Narratives* (Boston: Beacon Press, 1969), 256.
30. Jacobs, 116.
31. Ibid., 87.
32. See earlier discussion of Douglass and Tubman.
33. Jacobs, 98. Italics mine.
34. Newbell Niles Puckett, *Folk Beliefs of The Southern Negro* (Chapel Hill: The University of North Carolina Press, 1926), 388. Italics mine.
35. Robert Farris Thompson, *Flash of the Spirit: African & Afro-American Art & Philosophy* (New York: First Vintage, 1984), 55.
36. Jacobs, 93.
37. Georgia Writers Project, *Drums and Shadows*, 41.
38. Melville and Frances S. Herskovits, *Suriname Folk-Lore* (New York and London: Whittlesey House, 1934), 53.
39. Thompson, 12–16.
40. Ibid., 43.
41. Also commenting on the Yoruba Stephen Farrow noted that "a stronger 'medicine' is employed to overcome or counteract, an evil one, or a curse through a broken ewo ('taboo'), *Faith, Fancies and Fetich* (New York and Toronto: The Macmillan Co., 1926), 121.
42. There is also evidence in Henry Bibb's narrative that the idea of "Flying" existed in his home state of Kentucky. After being carted to Louisville after he was captured by four slave-hunters for an attempted escape, Bibb was briefly left in the care of slaveholder Daniel Lane. The man was notorious for his "slave selling, kidnapping, and negro hunting." As soon as he turned his back on his prisoner, Bibb with no hesitation seized the opportunity and took off. Yet few believed Lane's account of Bibb's escape: "Dan imputed my escape to my godliness! He said that I must have gone up in a chariot of fire, for I went off by flying; and that he should never again have anything to do with a praying negro." That Lane connected flight with the spirituality of slaves can likely be attributed to his familiarity with the customs of Igbo and others who subscribed to their notion of "flying Africans." Bibb, 73–79.
43. Jacobs, 156.
44. Beardslee quotes Stuckey: "As Stuckey tells us, in *Slave Culture*, many African communities believed 'if the deceased lived a good life, death, a mere crossing over the threshold into another world, was a precondition for being carried back into the mainstream of the living, in the name and body of grandchildren of succeeding generations." Beardslee, 1; see Stuckey, *Slave Culture*, 12.
45. Bradford, *Tubman*, 25–30, 114.
46. Ira Reid, "The John Canoe Festival," in *Phylon* 3, (1942): 365.
47. Ibid., 350.
48. Jacobs, 95.
49. Reid, 358.
50. Michael Gomez, *Exchanging Our Country Marks: The Transformation of African Identities in the Colonial and Antebellum South* (Chapel Hill: University of North Carolina Press, 1998), 22.
51. Edward Warren, *A Doctor's Experiences on Three Continents* (Baltimore: Cushings and Baily, 1885), 201; Stuckey, *Slave Culture: Nationalist Theory and the Foundations of Black America* (New York: Oxford University Press, 1987) 70–71. Stuckey's treatment of Sojourner Turth's remarks on the Pinkster festival in upstate New York demonstrates that African inspired parades like John Kuner were not limited to the South. Pinkster also occurred during the Christmas season. When Europeans brought the

tradition with them to New York slaves infused the festival with African elements. An African "king" was chosen to lead the procession that was accompanied with slave singing, dancing, drumming and fiddling. Stuckey draws comparisons between the celebration and the African New England parade of governors and the Cuban parade of Kings. In each of the carnivals there was dancing done in honor of an African "King" who was the focal point of the festival. Sojourner Truth, *Narrative of Sojourner Truth (the 1850 Text)*, ed. Margaret Washington (New York: Vintage, 1993), xxv, 48; Stuckey, 80, 142.

52. Stuckey, 70.
53. Stuckey, 68–69.
54. Beardslee, 2.
55. Reid, 350, 359; Dougald MacMillian, "John Kuners," in *The Journal of American Folklore* 39, no. 151 (Jan.-Mar., 1926): 55; Nancy R. Ping, "Black Musical Activities in Antebellum Wilmington, North Carolina," in *The Black Perspective in Music* (1980): 139.
56. Jacob Stroyer, "My Life in the South," in William Loren Katz, eds., *Five Slave Narratives* (New York: Arno Press, 1969), 45.
57. Stuckey, 19–20.
58. Charles Ball, *Fifty Years in Chains; or, The Life of an American Slave* (Indiana: Dayton & Asher, 1858), 140.
59. Ibid., 198.
60. Robert Smith, "The Canoe in West African History," in *The Journal of African History* 11, no. 4 (1970): 520.
61. Ibid., 525.
62. Reid, 365.
63. Smith, 522, 528.
64. Douglad MacMillian, *John Kuners*, 55.
65. Ibid., 54.
66. Reid, 350.
67. Martha Warren Beckwith, *Jamaica Folk-Lore* (New York: Kraus, 1969), 14.
68. In 1830 travelers R. and J. Lander included a drawing of an "'Iboe Canoe' with about twenty-two men engaged in paddling, two standing in the bows and stern with long poles as steersmen, and a platform amidships on which three warriors are standing." (possibly insert in footnote 518, ftn 21); Mungo Park witnessed a Bambara canoe carrying "four horses and several people across the river." Smith, 523.
69. Gomez, 140.
70. Peter Gutkind, "The Canoemen of the Gold Coast (Ghana)," in A Survey and an Exploration in Precolonial African Labour History," in *Cahiers d'études africaines* 29, no. 3, 4 (1989): 359.
71. Ibid., 349.
72. Ibid., 364–365.
73. Jacobs, 94.
74. Ibid., 14.
75. See earlier discussion of Brown and Douglass.
76. Jacobs, *Incidents* (Harvard 2000 edition), xv.
77. Jacobs, 9.
78. Ibid., 68.
79. Ibid., 70.
80. Ibid., 122.
81. Ibid., 12.
82. Ibid., 11.

83. Ibid., 62; For Wells' Brown critique of Adams see William Farrison, *William Wells Brown: Author & Reformer* (Chicago: University of Chicago, 1969), 254.
84. Jacobs, 62.
85. Jean Yellin, *Harriet Jacobs: A Life* (New York: Basic Civitas, 2004), 67–70.
86. Ibid., xix, 103–104.

NOTES TO CHAPTER 5

1. U.B. Phillips, *Life and Labor in the Old South* (Boston: Little, Brown, and Company, 1929), 219.
2. Marion Starling, *The Slave Narrative: Its Place in American History* (G. K. Hall & Co. Publishers, 1981; repr.; Washington, D.C.: Howard University Press, 1988), xiv.
3. Ibid., ix.
4. Ibid., 50.
5. Ibid., x; Kenneth M. Stampp, *The Peculiar Institution: Slavery in the Ante-Bellum South* (New York: Alfred A. Knopf, 1956; repr.; 1968), 60, 73, 74, 79, 127, 132, 162, 170, 176, 287, 291, 331.
6. Stanley Elkins, *Slavery: A Problem in American Institutional and Intellectual Life* (Chicago: University of Chicago Press, 1959), 3–5. It should be noted that Elkins, in the third edition to his book, conceded that there was some merit to be found in the new studies on slave folklore. He writes: "I am particulary intrigued by the conceptual possibilities Bryce-Laporte has outlined—to which should be added the findings Sterling Stuckey on slave folklore—for an 'underlife,' a subculture of great richness and variety. The suggestions of Bryce-Laporte and others on music, conjuring, prayer meetings, and escape lore, the descriptions of Negro night life in the cities by Richard Wade, Stuckey's studies of double meanings in work songs, spirituals, and the Brer Rabbit cycle—all thse represent a vast treasury of materials still waiting to be mined." See *Slavery: A Problem in American Institutional and Intellectual Life* (Chiago and London: The University of Chicago Press, 1976), 248–249.
7. Gilbert Osofsky, *Puttin' on ole Massa: The Slave Narratives of Henry Bibb, William Wells Brown and Solomon Northup* (New York: Harper & Row, 1969), 12.
8. Ibid., 38.
9. Ibid., 37.
10. Ibid., 38.
11. Arna Bontemps, *Great Slave Narratives* (Boston: Beacon Press, 1969), xvi.
12. Ibid., xviii.
13. Eugene Genovese, *Roll, Jordan, Roll: The World the Slaves Made* (New York: Random House, 1972).
14. John Blassingame, *The Slave Community: Plantation Life in the Antebellum South* (New York: Oxford University Press, 1972), 262.
15. John Blassingame, eds., *Slave Testimony: Two Centuries of Letters, Speeches, Interviews and Autobiographies* (Baton Rouge, Louisiana University Press, 1977), xlviii.
16. Ibid., xliii; Blassingame, *The Slave Community* 375–379.
17. Blassingame, *The Slave Community*, 376. Here the term "slave culture" is borrowed from Sterling Stuckey. See Stuckey, *Slave Culture: Nationalist Theory & The Foundation of Black America* (New York and Oxford: Oxford University Press, 1987).

18. Genovese, 218–223.
19. Blassingame maintains that these authors "learned much of African customs and languages from their African-born relatives. Others sometimes saw freshly imported Africans in the South in the 1840s and 50s." Blassingame, *The Slave Community*, 27–32.
20. George Rawick, eds., *The American Slave: A Composite Autobiography* (Connecticut: Greenwood, 1972–1979).
21. Alex Lichtenstein, "In Retrospect: George Rawick's From Sundown to Sunup and the Dialectic of Marxian Slave Studies." In *Reviews in American History* 24.4 (1996) 712–725.
22. George Rawick, *From Sunup to Sundown: The Making of the Black Community* (Connecticut: Greenwood, 1972), 159. Rawick also relates that "the abolitionist movement was essentially a product of the black community, although whites played a role in it. Abolitionism was at all times dominated by Afro-American freedmen, not by whites, although the inherent racism of American ideology has obscured that fact not only for most whites—with the notable exceptions of such men as James Wentworth Higginson and Wendell Phillips—who participated in the movement." Ibid., 111.
23. Ibid., 9, 99–110.
24. Lichtenstein, 712–725.
25. Stephen Butterfield, *Black Autobiography in America* (Amherst: University of Massachusetts Press, 1974), 15–16, 30, 52.
26. Ibid., 39.
27. Ibid., 40.
28. Ibid., 54–56.
29. Ibid., 26.
30. Robert Stepto, *From Behind the Veil: A Study of Afro-American Narrative* (Urbana: University of Illinois Press, 1979), 3–10.
31. Ibid., 4, 14.
32. Ibid., 20–23.
33. Ibid., 27.
34. Henry Louis Gates, Jr. and Charles T. Davis echoed these sentiments sixteen years later in their edited volume *The Slave's Narrative* (Oxford and New York: Oxford University Press, 1985), xxxiii, 168. The "talking book," according to Gates, appears not only in the narratives of John Marrant, Cugoano, Equiano, and John Jea but also in the writings of twentieth-century blacks, xxvii. Gates historicizes the genre by providing evidence to suggest that the slave narratives emerged largely as response to eighteenth- and nineteenth-century notions that blacks were devoid of the intellectual capacity to create literature worthy of serious recognition, xii, xv. Gates does not locate African cultural influences in the genre.
35. Stepto, 103.
36. William Andrews, "The First Fifty Years of the Slave Narrative," in John Sekora and Darwin Turner, eds., *The Art of Slave Narrative: Original Essays in Criticism and Theory* (Western Illinois: University Press, 1982), 8, 19. It should be noted that Olaudah Equiano and Venture Smith were African-born slaves who authored texts during the early period and each of their narratives include references to the religious and spiritual world from which they came. Olaudah Equinao, *The Interesting Narrative of the Life of Olaudah Equiano, or Gustavus Vass, The African Written by Himself*, vol. 1 (New York: W. Duell, 1791); Venture Smith, *A Narrative of the Life and Adventures of Venture, A Native of Africa; But Resident above Sixty Years in the United States of America, Related by Himself* (New London: C. Holt, 1798).

37. Annette Niemtzow, "The Problematic Self in Autobiography," in Ibid., 99–101.
38. Ibid., 106.
39. Frederick Douglass, "Life and Times of Frederick Douglass" (1893; repr.; *Douglass Autobiographies*, New York: Penguin, 1994), 490.
40. Harriet Jacobs, *Incidents in the Life of a Slave Girl: Contexts and Criticism.* ed., by Nellie Y. Mckay and Frances Smith Foster. (New York and London: W.W. Norton & Company, 2001), 95.
41. Sterling Stuckey, *Slave Culture: Nationalist Theory and the Foundations of Black America* (New York and Oxford: Oxford University Press, 1987), 3.
42. Peter Kolchin, *Unfree Labor: American Slavery and Russian Serfdom* (Cambridge: Belknap, 1987), 227–228.
43. Sterling Stuckey, "'Ironic Tenacity': Frederick Douglass's Seizure of the Dialectic," in Eric Sundquist's, eds., *Frederick Douglass: New Literary and Historical Essays* (Cambridge: University Press, 1990), 23–41.
44. Sterling Bland Jr., *Voices of the Fugitives: Runaway Slave Stories and their Stories of Self-Creation* (Connecticut: Praeger, 2000), 25–26.
45. Ibid., 109.
46. Patrick Rael, *Black Identity & Black Protest in the Antebellum North* (Chapel Hill and London: University of North Carolina Press, 2002), 129.
47. Ibid., 46–48, 129.
48. Sylvia Frey, *Water from the Rock: Black Resistance in a Revolutionary Age* (New Jersey: Princeton University Press, 1991), 87.
49. Benjamin Quarles, *Black Abolitionists* (New York: Oxford University Press, 1969); Jane & William H. Pease, *They who would be Free: Blacks' Search for Freedom, 1830–1861* (New York: Atheneum, 1974); Herbert Aptheker, *The Negro in the Abolitionist Movement* (New York: International Papers, 1941). Merton L. Dillon, *Slavery Attacked: Southern Slaves and their Allies, 1619–1865* (Baton Rouge & London: Louisiana State University Press, 1990); Paul Goodman, *Of One Blood: Abolitionism and the Origins of Racial Equality* (Berkeley: University of California Press, 1998).
50. Gilbert H Barnes, *The Antislavery Impulse, 1830–1944* (Massachusetts: P. Smith, 1933).
51. John R. McKivigan, eds., *History of the American Abolitionist Movement: A Bibliography of Scholarly Articles.* (Indianapolis: Indiana University, xv.) 1999. See David B. Davis, *The Problem of Slavery in Western Culture* (New York: Cornell University Press, 1966); Stanley Elkins, *Slavery: A problem in American Institutional Life* (Chicago: University of Chicago Press, 1959); Hugh Davis, *Joshua Leavitt, Evangelical abolitionist* (Baton Rouge: Louisiana State University Press, 1990); Victor B. Howard, *Conscience and Slavery: The Evangelistic Calvinist Domestic Missions, 1837–1861* (Kent, Ohio: Kent State University Press, 1990); Merton L. Dillon, *Slavery Attacked: Southern Slaves and Their Allies, 1619–1990* (Baton Rouge & London: Louisiana State University Press, 1990).
52. Often desired for their expertise in rice cultivation Senegambians were significantly represented in South Carolina. Virginia, Maryland, and Louisiana also enjoyed a fair contingent. According to Mike Gomez, the Bambara of Senegambia developed quite a reputation for rebelling in America. They were also known to have relied on sacred amulets. Mike Gomez, *Exchanging Our Country Marks: The Transformation of African Identity in the Colonial and Antebellum South* (Chapel Hill: University of North Carolina Press, 1998). For further discussion on the Senegambian presence in America see Gwendolyn Midlo Hall, *Africans in Colonial Louisiana: The Development of Afro-Creole Culture in the Eighteenth Century* (Baton Rouge: Louisiana

State University Press, 1992). Also important are Elizabeth Donnan, *Documents Illustrative of the History of the Slave Trade to America* (New York: Octagon, 1965); Phillip Curtin, *Economic Change in Precolonial Africa: Senegambia in the Era of the Slave Trade* (Madison: University of Wisconsin Press, 1975); Boubacar Barry, *Senegambia and the Atlantic Slave Trade* (Cambridge: Cambridge University Press, 1998); Michael Gomez, *Pragmatism in The Age of Jihad: The Precolonial State of Bundu* (Cambridge: Cambridge University Press, 1992).

53. James Currey, ed., *General History of Africa: Africa from the Sixteenth to the Eighteenth Century* (California: UNESCO, 1990) vol. 5, [abridged edition], 134–152.
54. Gomez, *Exchanging Our Country Marks*, 63.
55. Gomez, *Pragmatism in the Age of the Jihad*, 49.
56. The Europeans called it the Toubenan movement while it was known to the Berbers as the Shurbuba movement. Barry, 53.
57. Gomez, *Pragmatisim in the Age of Jihad*, 48–51.
58. John Thornton attributes the royalist sentiments of Haitian revolutionaries to Kongo political ideology. "African Soldiers in the Haitian Revolution," *Journal of Caribbean History*, 25 (1991): 58–80.
59. Gomez, 29.
60. Gomez points out that "although the contribution of Senegambia to the trade declined dramatically after 1750, the combined evidence suggests that the bulk of the captives came from the midrange to upper- and middle-Niger areas, in which Islam was relatively more widespread." Gomez, *Exchanging Our Country Marks*, 64.
61. Herbert Aptheker, *American Negro Slave Revolts* (New York: International Publishers, 1963), 173.
62. Aptheker writes of several slave plots and conspiracies that took place in the North from the 1690s to the 1780s, 162–208.
63. Gwendolyn Midlo Hall, *Africans in Colonial Louisiana: The Development of Afro-Creole Culture in the Eighteenth Century* (Baton Rouge: Louisiana State Unviersity Press, 1992).
64. Hall drafted petitions in 1773, 1774, 1777 and 1778. See Charles H. Wesley, *Prince Hall: Life and Legacy* (Washington: United Supreme Council, 1977), 63–69.
65. "Petition of Prince Hall and Other Blacks, January 13, 1777," Massachusetts Archives, Massachusetts Division of Archives, Boston, Mass., as reprinted in *Massachusetts Historical Collections*, Series 5, 3: 436- 37. This revolutionary sentiment was built off the many conspiracies and revolts of the early period (Stono, NY. Etc). There were also articles written by blacks signed "othello" and "a free Negro" in 1788 and 1789 denouncing slavery and demanding the realization in practice of the declaration of independence.
66. Starling, 50.
67. William L. Andrews, *To Tell a Free Story: The First Century of Afro-American Autobiography, 1760–1865* (Urbana: University of Illinois Press, 1986).
68. Valerie Smith, *Self Discovery and Authority in Afro-American Narrative* (Cambridge: Harvard University Press, 1987).

Bibliography

PRIMARY SOURCES:

Ball, Charles. *Fifty Years in Chains; or, The Life of an American Slave.* Indianapolis, Indiana: Dayton & Asher, 1858.

Bibb, Henry. *The Life and Adventures of Henry Bibb: An American Slave*, Introduction by Charles Heglar. New York 2001.

Blassingame, John ed. *Slave Testimony: Two Centuries of Letters, Speeches, Interviews and Autobiographies.* Baton Rouge: Louisiana University Press, 1977.

———, ed. *The Frederick Douglass Papers.* New Haven: Yale University Press, 1979.

Bontemps, Arna, ed. *Great Slave Narratives.* Boston: Beacon Press, 1969.

Bosman, William. *Description of the Coast of Guinea.* London: F. Knapton, 1705.

Bowdich, T. E. *Mission to Cape Coast Castle and Ashantee.* London: Frank Cass & Co., 1966.

Bradford, Sarah H. *Scenes in the Life of Harriet Tubman.* Auburn, N.Y.: W.J. Moses, 1869.

———. *Harriet Tubman, the Moses of Her People.* Bedford, Applewood Books, 1993.

Bremer, Fredrika. *America of the Fifties: Letters of Fredrika.* New York: Oxford University Press, 1924.

Brown, William Wells. *The Anti-Slavery Harp: A Collection of Songs for Anti-Slavery Meetings.* Boston: Bela Marsh, 1848.

———. *The Black Man, His Antecedents, His Genius, and His Achievements.* New York: Arno Press, 1969.

———. *Clotel; or, The President's Daughter. With a Sketch of the Author's Life.* In *Three Classic African-American Novels*, edited by Henry Louis Gates, Jr. New York: Vintage Classics, 1990.

———. *The Escape; Or, A Leap For Freedom: A Drama in Five Acts.* Knoxville: University of Tennessee Press, 2001.

———. *My Southern Home: Or, The South and Its People.* Boston: A. G. Brown & Co., Publishers, 1880.

———. *Narrative of William W. Brown, a Fugitive Slave, Written by Himself*, in *Five Slave Narratives*, William Loren Katz. New York: Arno, 1968.

———. *The Rising Son; or, The Antecedents and Advancement of the Colored Race.* Miami: Mnemosyne Inc., 1969.

Burton, Richard. *A Mission to Gelele, King of Dahomey.* London: Tinsley Brothers, 1864.

Cheney, Ednah Dow Littlehale. "Moses." *Freedmen's Record.* March (1865).

Douglass, Frederick. "My Bondage and My Freedom." *Douglass Autobiographies.* New York: Penguin, 1994.

————. "Life and Times of Frederick Douglass." *Douglass Autobiographies*. New York: Penguin, 1994.

————. "Narrative of the Life of Frederick Douglass, An American Slave." *Douglass Autobiographies*, New York: Penguin, 1994.

Drew, Benjamin. "The Refugee: A North-Side View of Slavery." In *Four Fugitive Slave Narratives*, Introduction by Robin Winks. Reading, Massachusetts: Addison-Wesley, 1969.

Dubois, W.E.B. "The Souls of Black Folk," in *Three Negro Classics*, edited byJohn Hope Franklin, 207–389. New York: Avon Books, 1963.

Georgia Writer's Project. *Drums and Shadows*. Athens, Georgia: The University of Georgia Press, 1940.

Higginson, Thomas W. *Army Life in a Black Regiment*. Boston: Lee and Shepard, 1890.

Holt, Rosa Belle. "A Heroine in Ebony." *Chautauquan* 23: 459–462, 1886.

Hurston, Zora Neale. *Moses: Man of the Mountain*. New York: Harper Collins, 1967.

————. *Tell My Horse: Voodoo and Life in Haiti and Jamaica*. New York: Harper and Row, 1990.

————. *Mules and Men*. New York: Harper and Row, 1990.

Hyatt, Harry Middleton. *Hoodoo, Conjuration, Witchcraft, Rootwork*. Sappinton, Missouri: Western Publishing, 1970.

Isert, Paul Erdmann. *Letters On West Africa And The Slave Trade: Paul Erdmann Isert's Journey to Guinea and the Caribbean Islands in Columbia*. New York: Oxford University Press, 1992.

Jacobs, Harriet. *Incidents in the Life of a Slave Girl [by] Linda Brent*. New York: Harcourt Brace Jovanovich, 1973.

————. *Incidents in the Life of A Slave Girl*. New York and London: Norton, 2001.

Payne, Daniel. *Recollections of Seventy Years*. New York: Arno Press, 1968.

Pennington, James W. C. "The Fugitive Blacksmith," in *Great Slave narratives*, edited by Arna Bontemps. Boston: Beacon Press, 1969.

"Petition of Prince Hall and Other Blacks, January 13, 1777," Massachusetts Archives, Massachusetts Division of Archives, Boston, MA., as reprinted in *Massachusetts Historical Collections* 5: 436–437, 1967.

Rawick, George, eds. *The American Slave: A Composite Autobiography*. Westport, Connecticut: Greenwood, 1972–1979.

Ripley, C. Peter, ed., *The Black Abolitionist Papers*. Chapel Hill: University of North Carolina, 1985–1992.

Sanborn, Franklin. "Harriet Tubman." *The Commonwealth*, July 17 (1863).

Stroyer, Jacob, "My Life in the South," in *Five Slave Narratives*, edited byWilliam Loren Katz. New York: Arno, 1969.

Truth, Sojourner. *Narrative of Sojourner Truth*, edited by Margaret Washington. New York: Vintage, 1993.

Warren, Edward. *A Doctor's Experiences on Three Continents*. Baltimore: Cushings and Baily, 1885.

Yellin, Jean, ed. *Incidents in the Life of a Slave Girl*. Cambridge: Harvard University Press, 1987.

SECONDARY SOURCES:

Andrews, William L. "The First Fifty Years of the Slave Narrative," in *The Art of Slave Narrative: Original Essays in Criticism and Theory*, edited by John Sekora and Darwin Turner. Urbana: University Press, 1982.

———. *To Tell a Free Story: The First Century of Afro-American Autobiography, 1760–1865.* Urbana: University of Illinois Press, 1986.

———. *From Fugitive Slave to Free man: The Autobiographies of William Wells Brown.* Columbia: University of Missouri Press, 2003.

Aptheker, Herbert. *The Negro in the Abolitionist Movement.* New York: International Papers, 1941.

Barnes, Gilbert H. *The Antislavery Impulse, 1830–1944.* New York: D. Appleton-Century Company, 1933.

Barry, Boubacar. *Senegambia and the Atlantic Slave Trade.* Cambridge, UK: Cambridge University Press, 1998.

Basden, George Thomas. *Among the Ibos of Nigeria.* Philadelphia: J. B. Lippincott Co., 1931.

Beardslee, Karen. "Through Slave Culture's Lens Comes the Abundant Source: Harriet A. Jacobs's Incidents in the Life of a Slave Girl—Critical Essay." *Melus* Spring (1999).

Beckwith, Martha. *Black Roadways.* Chapel Hill: The University of North Carolina Press, 1929.

Bland Jr., Sterling. *Voices of the Fugitives: Runaway Slave Stories and their Stories of Self-Creation.* Westport: Praeger, 2000.

Blassingame, John. *The Slave Community: Plantation Life in the Antebellum South.* New York: Oxford University Press, 1972.

Bontemps, Arna ed. *Black Thunder.* Boston: Beacon, 1968.

Burnham, Michelle. "Loopholes of Resistance: Harriet Jacobs' Slave Narrative and the Critique of Agency in Foucault." *Arizona Quarterly* 49.2 (1993): 53–73.

Butterfield, Stephen. *Black Autobiography in America.* Amherst: University of Massachusetts Press, 1974.

Clinton, Catherine. *Harriet Tubman: The Road to Freedom.* New York and Boston: Little, Brown and Company, 2004.

Conrad, Earl. *Harriet Tubman.* Washington, D.C.: The Associated Publishers, 1943.

Courlander, Harold. *A Treasury of African Folklore: The Oral Literature, Traditions, Myths, Legends, Epics, Tales, Recollections, Wisdom, Sayings, and Humor of Africa.* New York: Crown Publishers, 1975.

Currey, James, ed. *General History of Africa: Africa from the Sixteenth to the Eighteenth Century.* San Francisco: UNESCO, 1990. [abridged edition].

Curtin, Phillip. *Economic Change in Precolonial Africa: Senegambia in the era of the Slave Trade.* Madison: University of Wisconsin Press, 1975.

Davies, Hunter. *William Wordsworth: A Biography.* New York: Atheneum, 1980.

Davis, David B. *The Problem of Slavery in Western Culture.* New York: Cornell University Press, 1966.

Davis, Hugh. *Joshua Leavitt, Evangelical Abolitionist.* Baton Rouge: Louisiana State University Press, 1990.

Diagne, P. "African Political, Economic and Social Structures During this Period." In *Africa from the Sixteenth to the Eighteenth Century*, edited by B.A. Ogot, 26–34. London: Heinemann; Berkeley, University of California Press, Paris: UNESCO, 1992.

Dillon, Merton L. *Slavery Attacked: Southern Slaves and their Allies, 1619–1865.* Baton Rouge & London: Louisiana State University Press, 1990.

Donnan, Elizabeth Donnan. *Documents Illustrative of the History of the Slave Trade to America.* New York: Octagon, 1965.

Elkins, Stanley. *Slavery: A Problem in American Institutional Life.* Chicago: University of Chicago Press, 1959.

Ellis, A. B. *The Tshi-Speaking Peoples of the Slave Coast of West Africa.* London: Chapman & Hall, Ltd., 1887.

————. *The Yoruba-Speaking Peoples of the Slave Coast of West Africa*. London: Chapman & Hall, Ltd., 1894.

Ephirim-Donkor, Anthony. *African Spirituality: On Becoming Ancestors*. Lawrenceville: Africa World Press, 1997.

Farrison, William. *William Wells Brown: Author & Reformer*. Chicago: University of Chicago Press, 1969.

Farrow, Stephen. *Faith, Fancies and Fetich*. New York and Toronto: The Macmillan Co., 1926.

Faulkner, William John. *The Days When the Animals Talked*. Chicago: Follette Publishers, 1977.

Foner, Phillip. *Frederick Douglass, A Biography*. New York: Citadel, 1964.

Frey, Sylvia. *Water from the Rock: Black Resistance in a Revolutionary Age*. Princeton: Princeton University Press, 1991.

Gates, Henry Louis and Davis, Charles T, ed. *The Slave's Narrative*. Oxford and New York: Oxford University Press, 1985.

Genovese, Genovese. *Roll, Jordan, Roll: The World the Slaves Made*. New York: Random House, 1972.

Gomez, Michael. *Pragmatism in The Age of Jihad: The Precolonial State of Bundu*. Cambridge, UK: Cambridge University Press, 1992.

————. *Exchanging Our Country Marks*. Chapel Hill: University of North Carolina Press, 1998.

Gonza'lez-Wippler, Migene. *The New Revised Sixth and Seventh Books of Moses and the Magical Uses of the Psalms*. New York: Original Publications, 1991.

Goodman, Paul. *Of One Blood: Abolitionism and the Origins of Racial Equality*. Berkeley: University of California Press, 1998.

Gunning, Sandra. "Reading and Redemption in *Incidents in the Life of a Slave Girl*," in *Harriet Jacobs and Incidents in the Life of a Slave Girl: New Critical Essays*, edited by Deborah M. Garfield and Rafia Zafar, 131–154. New York: Cambridge University Press, 1996.

Gutkind, Peter. "The Canoemen of the Gold Coast (Ghana)." *Cahiers d'études africaines* 29 (1989): 359.

Hall, Gwendolyn Midlo. *Africans in Colonial Louisiana: The Development of Afro-Creole Culture in the Eighteenth Century*. Baton Rouge: Louisiana State University Press, 1992.

Harold, Stanley. *American Abolitionists*. New York: Longman, 2001.

Heermance, J. Noel. *William Wells Brown and Clotelle: A Portrait of the Artist in the First Negro Novel*. North Haven: Shoe String, 1969.

Herskovits, Melville and Frances S. *Suriname Folk-Lore*. New York and London: Whittlesey House, 1934.

Herskovits, Melville. *Life in a Haitian Valley*. New York and London: Knoph, 1937.

————. *Dahomey*. New York: J. J. Augustin, 1938.

Howard, Victor B. *Conscience and Slavery: The Evangelistic Calvinist Domestic Missions, 1837–1861*. Kent, OH: Kent State University Press, 1990.

Humez, Jean M. *Harriet Tubman: The Life and the Life Stories*. Madison: The University of Wisconsin Press, 2003.

Jefferson, Paul, ed. *The Travels of William Wells Brown*. New York: Markus Wiener, 1991.

————. *First Freedom: The Responses of Alabama's Blacks to Emancipation and Reconstruction*. Westport: Greenwood Press, 1972.

Kolchin, Peter. *Unfree Labor: American Slavery and Russian Serfdom*. Cambridge: Belknap, 1987.

Larson, Kate C. *Bound For The Promise Land: Harriet Tubman, Portrait of An American Hero*. New York: Random House, 2004.

Leonard, Major Arthur Glyn. *The Lower Niger and Its Tribes*. New York: The Macmillan Co., 1906.

Levine, Lawrence. *Black Culture and Black Consciousness*. New York: Oxford University Press, 1977.

Lichtenstein, Alex. "In Retrospect: George Rawick's From Sundown to Sunup and the Dialectic of Marxian Slave Studies." *Reviews in American History* 24.4 (1996): 712–725.

MacMillian Dougald. "John Kuners." *The Journal of American Folklore* 39 (1926): 55.

Martin Jr., Waldo. *The Mind of Frederick Douglass*. Chapel Hill and London: UNC Press, 1984.

McFeely, William. *Frederick Douglass*. New York: Norton, 1991.

Mckay, Nellie Y. "The Girls Who Became the Women: Childhood Memories in the Autobiographies of Harriet Jacobs, Mary Church Terrell, and Anne Moody," in *Tradition and the Talents of Women*, edited by Florence Howe, 106–124. Urbana and Chicago: University of Illinois Press, 1991.

McKay, Nellie Y and Foster, Frances Smith, ed. *Incidents in the Life of a Slave Girl: Contexts and Criticisms*. New York and London: W. W. Norton & Company, 2001.

McKivigan, John R., ed. *History of the American Abolitionist Movement: A Bibliography of Scholarly Articles*. Indianapolis: Indiana University, 1999.

Meek, C.K. *A Sudanese Kingdom and Ethnographical Study of the Jukun-Speaking Peoples of Nigeria*. London: Kegan, 1931.

———. *Law and Authority in a Nigerian Tribe*. London: Oxford University Press, 1937.

Menzies, Alan. *History of Religion: A Sketch of Primitive Religious Beliefs and Practices and of the Origin and Character of the Great Systems*. New York: Scribner's Sons, 1897.

Milligan, Robert Milligan. *The Fetish Folk of West Africa*. New York: Fleming H. Revell Co., 1912.

Morley, John. Introduction to *The Complete Poetical Works of William Wordsworth*. New York: Thomas Y. Crowell Company Publishers, 1907.

Nassau, Robert Hamill. *Fetichism in West Africa*. New York: Charles Scribner's Sons, 1904.

Niemtzow, Annette. "The Problematic Self in Autobiography," in *The Art of Slave Narrative: Original Essays in Criticism and Theory*, edited by John Sekora and Darwin Turner, 99–101. Urbana: University Press, 1982.

O'Meally, Robert G. "The Vernacular Tradition," in *The Norton Anthology to African American Literature*, edited by Henry Louis Gates Jr., 1–4. New York: W. W. Norton & Co., 1997.

Osofsky, Gilbert. *Puttin' on ole Massa: The Slave Narratives of Henry Bibb, William Wells Brown and Solomon Northup*. New York: Harper & Row, 1969.

Painter, Nell Irvin. "Three Southern Women and Freud: A Non-Exceptionalist Approach to Race, Class, and Gender in the Slave South," in *Feminists Revision History*, edited by Ann-Louise, 195–216. New Brunswick: Rutgers University Press, 1994.

Parrish, Lydia. *Slave Songs of the Georgia Sea Islands*. New York: Creative Age Press, 1942.

Pease, Jane and William H. *They Who Would be Free: Blacks' Search for Freedom, 1830–1861*. New York: Atheneum, 1974.

Phillippo, James M. *Jamaica, Past and Present*. London: J. Snow, 1843.

Phillips, U. B. *Life and Labor in the Old South*. Boston: Little, Brown, and Company, 1929.

Ping, Nancy R. "Black Musical Activities in Antebellum Wilmington, North Carolina." *The Black Perspective in Music* (1980): 139.

Preston, Dickson J. *Young Frederick Douglass.* London: John Hopkins, 1980.

Puckett, Newbell Niles. *Folk Beliefs of The Southern Negro.* Chapel Hill: The University of North Carolina Press, 1926.

Quarles, Benjamin. *Frederick Douglass.* Washington, D.C.: Associated Publishers, 1948.

———. *Black Abolitionists.* New York: Oxford University Press, 1969.

Rael, Patrick. *Black Identity & Black Protest in the Antebellum North.* Chapel Hill and London: University of North Carolina Press, 2002.

Rattray, Robert. *Ashanti Proverbs.* Oxford, UK: The Clarendon Press, 1930.

———. *From Sunup to Sundown: The Making of the Black Community.* Westport: Greenwood, 1972.

Reid, Ira. "The John Canoe Festival." *Phylon* 3 (1942): 365.

Smith, Robert. "The Canoe in West African History." *The Journal of African History* 11 (1970): 520.

Smith, Theophus H. *Conjuring Culture.* New York and Oxford: Oxford University Press, 1994.

Smith, Valerie. *Self Discovery and Authority in Afro-American Narrative.* Cambridge: Harvard University Press, 1987.

Stampp, Kenneth M. *The Peculiar Institution: Slavery in the Ante-Bellum South.* New York: Alfred A. Knopf, 1956.

Starling, Marion. *The Slave Narrative: Its Place in American History.* Washington, D.C.: Howard University Press, 1988.

Stepto, Robert. *From Behind the Veil: A Study of Afro-American Narrative.* Urbana: University of Illinois Press, 1979.

Stuckey, Sterling. *Slave Culture: Nationalist Theory and the Foundations of Black America.* New York: Oxford University Press, 1987.

———. "'Ironic Tenacity': Frederick Douglass's Seizure of the Dialectic," in *Frederick Douglass: New Literary and Historical Essays*, edited by Eric Sundquist, 23-41. Cambridge, UK: Cambridge University Press, 1990.

———. "The Tambourine in Glory," in *The Cambridge Companion to Herman Melville*, edited by Robert S. Levine, 57–63. New York: Cambridge University Press, 1998.

Swint, Henry L. Swint, ed. *Dear Ones at Home: Letters from Contraband Camps.* Nashville: Vanderbuilt University Press, 1966.

Talbot, Amaury, Percy. *Life in Southern Nigeria.* London: Oxford University Press, 1926.

Thompson, Robert Farris. *Flash of the Spirit: African & Afro-American Art & Philosophy.* New York: First Vintage, 1984.

Thornton, John. "African Soldiers in the Haitian Revolution." *Journal of Caribbean History* 25 (1991): 58–80.

The Trans-Atlantic Slave Trade: A Database on CD-Rom, edited by David Eltis, Stephen D. Behrendt, David Richardson and Herbert Klein. Cambridge, UK: Cambridge University Press, 1999.

Turner, Lorenzo D. *Africanisms in the Gullah Dialect.* Chicago: University of Chicago Press, 1949.

———. "Problems Confronting the Investigator of Gullah." *Publications of the American Dialect Society* 9 (1947): 74–84.

Walker, Juliet E. *The History of Black Business in America.* New York: Macmillan Press, 1998.

Welchel Jr., L. H. *My Chains Fell Off: William Wells Brown, Fugitive Abolitionist.* Lanham: University Press of America, 1985.

Wesley, Charles H. *Prince Hall: Life and Legacy.* Washington, D.C.: United Supreme Council, 1977.

Williamson, Scott C. *The Narrative Life: The Moral and Religious Thought of Frederick Douglass.* Macon: Mercer University Press, 2002.

Yellin, Jean. "Written by Herself: Harriet Jacobs' Slave Narrative." *American Literature* 53.3 (1981): 379–486.

———. *Harriet Jacobs: A Life.* New York: Basic Civitas Books, 2004.

Index

Note: Information presented in footnotes is indicated by an 'n' following the page number and preceding the note number.

T - #0147 - 270225 - C0 - 229/152/8 - PB - 9780415846097 - Gloss Lamination